Mimosa's Voyages:
Official Logs, Crew Lists and M_____

Mimosa's Voyages:

Official Logs, Crew Lists and Masters

Compiled and Edited by Susan Wilkinson

First impression: 2007
© Susan Wilkinson and Y Lolfa Cyf., 2007

Cover design: Y Lolfa

ISBN-13: 9 780 86243 983 5
ISBN-10: 0 86243 983 3

Printed on acid-free and partly recycled paper
and published and bound in Wales by
Y Lolfa Cyf., Talybont, Ceredigion SY24 5AP
e-mail ylolfa@ylolfa.com
website www.ylolfa.com
tel 01970 832 304
fax 832 782

Acknowledgements

The Official Logs and Crew Agreements pertaining to Mimosa's voyages and "runs" between home ports are held in the National Archives at Kew, the National Maritime Museum in Greenwich, the Liverpool Record Office and in the Maritime History Archives at Memorial University, St. John's, Newfoundland, copyright of which is held by the National Archives.

I am grateful to these institutions for giving permission to publish the Official Logs and Crew Agreements they hold.

The Official Log Book

Under the Merchant Shipping Act of 1854 masters of British merchant ships, except those vessels employed in trading between home ports, were required to keep an Official Log Book in the form sanctioned by the Board of Trade.

Every entry in the Official Log had to be made as soon as possible after the event to which it related occurred. Each entry was required to be signed by the Master and Mate or other member of the Crew. Such events requiring documentation were:

1. Desertion or refusal to join the ship without reasonable cause.

2. Every offense and legal conviction of any member of the crew and the punishment or fine inflicted.

3. Every case of illness or injury and the medical treatment adopted (if any).

4. Every death and its cause.

5. Births and marriages occurring on board..

5. The name of any Seaman or Apprentice who ceased to be a member of the ship's crew, with the place, time and manner by which the discharge or desertion occurred.

6. The sale of the effects of any member of the crew dying during the voyage, including a statement of each article sold and the wages due.

7. Collision with any other ship and the circumstance under which the event occurred.

Punishments for offenses:

Desertion: liable to imprisonment with or without hard labour, forfeiture of wages, clothes and effects left behind on board.

Refusal, without reasonable cause, to join the ship or proceed to sea, absence without leave within 24 hours of the ship's sailing time from any port either at the commencement or during the progress of a voyage, absence from duty not deemed desertion: imprisonment for a term not exceeding 10 weeks, with or without hard labour, forfeiture of wages.

Quitting the ship without leave after arrival at a port of delivery: forfeiture of wages not exceeding one month's pay.

Willful disobedience to any lawful command or continued willful neglect of duty, willfully damaging the ship or any of the stores or cargo: imprisonment for a period not exceeding 12 weeks, with or without hard labour.

Upon the commission of any act of misconduct for which a Seaman subjected himself to a fine, the entry made in the Official Log Book had to be read distinctly and audibly to the offender and his reply, if any, to be recorded.

It was further required that:

In the case of Foreign-going Ships, the Master should, within 48 hours of the Ship's arrival at the final port of destination in the United Kingdom or upon discharge of the crew the Official Log Book was to be delivered to the Shipping Master in the home port, before whom the crew was discharged.

If any ship ceased by reason of transfer of ownership or change of employment as a Foreign-going or Home Trade Ship, the Master or Owner was required to deliver to the Shipping Master of the Ship's home port the Official Log Book duly made out at the time at which the ship ceased to be a Foreign-going or Home Trade Ship.

The Agreement and Account of Crew

The Articles of Agreement was a contract between the shipowner and all officers and crew, binding them for the duration of the voyage which, on the voyages to China, were expected to be for three years. The Articles stipulated daily rations to be allocated to each man, the destination and probable length of the voyage, the wage per month to which each man was entitled. The name, age, place of birth, name of previous ship was entered, the date and time of boarding was entered. Each man signed his name, if he could, or a mark in the shape of a cross if he could not.

By signing the Articles of Agreement the crew agreed to conduct themselves in a sober and honest manner and to be diligent in their duties, obedient to the lawful commands of the Master and Superior Officers.

The signing was done in the Shipping Office of the home port or, in the cases of late arrivals, on board ship in the Master's cabin.

Master and Crew

The crew for a clipper of *Mimosa*'s size would have been at least twenty: master, mate, carpenter, boatswain or second mate, steward, cook, twelve able seamen and ordinary seamen, two or more boy apprentices.

The Master

The master was appointed by the owners. However well *Mimosa* was built and however fast she was designed to sail, once at sea she was entirely in the hands of her master upon whom her life depended, who would bestow upon her either greatness or ignominy.

Many masters were themselves part-owners, like Trevanion Huge, and had a financial interest in their ship's performance. A master had to have the confidence of the ship's owners since the ship was beyond the owners' direct control for long periods and, once at sea, beyond even the jurisdiction of English law. There were no official inquiries when men died either from natural causes or by falling overboard. Such incidents were merely recorded in the Official Log book together with a list of the dead man's possessions. Desertions and deaths were required to be reported to the local British consul in the port they occurred or the closest port after they occurred.

Although many owners employed the same master for a particular ship, keeping the one master for the ship's lifetime or until it was sold, every contract was for a single voyage, for most owners were not willing to keep a master on their payroll in the intervals between voyages. The one- or two-voyage master, like Archibald Johnson or the luckless Stephen Goodman, was not likely to be trusted with more than the handling of the crew and the navigation of the ship, the commercial matters in foreign ports being handled by an appointed agent who would instruct the master as to the owners' instructions.

The Mate

The mate needed to be a competent navigator so that he could take over the ship if the master died or, as sometimes occurred, had his command divested of him in a mutiny. The master sometimes deferred to the mate's superior navigational ability or to his knowledge of an unfamiliar coast or sea. The mate enforced the master's orders, often with physical force. The mate was in charge of the port watch and had first selection of the seamen to work the watches.

The Boatswain

The boatswain, bosun, or second mate was the petty officer who supervised the deck crew and the maintenance of the rigging and anchors. The starboard watch was under his command, often under the supervision of the master.

The Carpenter

The ship's carpenter had always served a seven-year apprenticeship, often as boy apprentice in a shipyard or, after a year or two in the yard, as a carpenter's mate at sea. He would have to know how to repair hulls and masts damaged in a storm and, in the event of a shipwreck, rebuild an entire ship with the help of some unskilled labour.

The Cook

The cook had no special training and was regarded as well below the carpenter in status. Often he had been an Able or Ordinary seaman who had been maimed or partially incapacitated in some accident. It was rare that a ship's cook had any particular culinary skill.

The Steward

The steward waited at the officers' table. He prepared and served the officers' meals, cleared and washed the dishes and kept the galley clean. He was also supposed to dust the master's cabin and polish the mahogany work and brass fittings. Having charge of the key to the cupboard where spirits were stored, the steward sometimes succumbed to temptation and became inebriated.

It was also the steward's duty to assist the surgeon, when there was one on board.

The Able and Ordinary Seamen

The Able seamen had to be "able" to "hand, reef and steer". The Ordinary seamen worked as deckhands. Many seamen were foreign-born and most were the dregs of whatever port they had signed on at, given to drunkenness, violence and foul language. They were hired by the voyage, often on the day of sailing; and when the voyage was over, they remained on shore after discharge, driven to look for other employment when their wages were spent or stolen, until they could sign on again on another ship.

Seamen were frequently crimped or "shanghaied" from taverns, brothels or the streets and delivered to a waiting ship. It is certain that many of *Mimosa*'s crews were crimped and deserted at the first opportunity.

The Apprentice

Apprentices were of three kinds:

Navigation apprentices were often the sons of minor merchants, tradesmen or master mariners who, in their three- or four-year voluntary apprenticeships, would be instructed in navigation and the skills of mastership so that one day they too might become masters or, at the very least, ships' officers. Depending on their family connections, their treatment and expectations varied. They were paid no wages; rather, a premium was demanded in return for the skills they were taught.

Ordinary apprentices were apprenticed to a master or mate and were maintained between ships and voyages when they were sent to earn wages in port which they were expected to hand over to their master. They were given some pay which increased a little year by year. After two or three years they would have been able to get employment first as Ordinary seamen and eventually as Able seamen.

Pauper apprentices were bound for sever or sometimes even nine years for which they were entitled to no pay. Their condition on board ship was miserable. Unlike paying apprentices, they were not trained to be officers and had no expectations beyond being trained to be Ordinary seamen or stewards.

The Surgeon and Purser

The surgeon, with their one or two assistants, indispensable for the two-year voyages of the East Indiamen and, for obvious reasons, in fighting ships of the Royal Navy, were not required for the faster clipper runs when no passengers were carried.

The purser, too, had vanished from the crew lists of merchant ships by the 19th century since the clerical work for which he had been hitherto employed was now done by literate masters who no longer signed their names with an "X", aided, when necessary, by agents ashore. On the rare occasions when a purser was employed his status was a lowly one.

There was one time when a surgeon and purser were employed on *Mimosa*. This was on her voyage to Patagonia.

The Supercargo

The supercargo, when on board, was not a member of the ship's crew. Often a relative of the owner and always a separate employee of the merchant whom he was representing, he handled the commercial side of the ship's trade affairs when in port. He could demand that a ship alter course, his orders superceding the authority of the master.

Mimosa's Masters and their Voyages and Runs

Thomas Kemp (C2797)

1. Aberdeen – Newcastle (in ballast)
    July 5, 1853 – July 19, 1853
    (National Archives, Kew, BT 98/3423)

2. North Shield – Rio de Janeiro
    July 28, 1853 – March 11, 1854
    (National Archives, BT 98/3423)

3. Run from Bristol – Liverpool
    March, 1854. (Documentation missing)

4. Liverpool – Shanghai
    June 8, 1854 – May 10, 1855
    (National Archives, BT 98/4205)

5. Liverpool – Shanghai
    June 5, 1855 – January 14, 1856
    (National Archives, BT 98/4546)

6. Liverpool to Shanghai
    February 19, 1856 – January 18, 1857
    (National Archives, BT 98/4788)

7. Run from London – Liverpool
    February 10, 1857 – February 17, 1857
    (National Archives, BT 98/4788)

8. Liverpool – Rio de Janeiro
    March 19, 1857 – October 10, 1857
    (National Archives, BT 98/4788)

Trevanion Hugo (C2797)

9. Liverpool – Rio de Janeiro
   November 17, 1857 – May 23, 1858
   (National Archives BT 98/5122)

10. Liverpool – Rio de Janeiro
    July 2, 1858 – November 23, 1858
    (National Archives, BT 98/5122)

11. Liverpool – Rio de Janeiro
    February 3, 1859 – August 1, 1859
    (National Archives, BT 98/5591)

12. Liverpool – Rio de Janeiro
    October 26, 1859 – April 25, 1860
    (National Archives, BT 98/6283)

13. Liverpool – Rio de Janeiro and Mauritius
    June 16, 1860 – January 28, 1861
    (National Maritime Museum, Greenwich, BE
    1529/1/2/3/62)

14. Run from Bristol – Liverpool
    February 11, 1861 – February 23, 1861
    (National Maritime Museum, BE
    1529/1/2/3/62)

15. Liverpool – Mauritius
    March 31, 1861 – October 15, 1861
    (National Maritime Museum, BE
    1529/1/2/3/62)

16. Liverpool – Rio de Janeiro
    December 2, 1861 – May 10, 1862
    (National Maritime Museum, BE
    1529/2/2/2/35)

Archibald Johnson (S71822)

17. Liverpool – Bahia
    July 14, 1862 – February 2, 1863
    (National Archives, BT 99/140)

18. Liverpool – Foochow
    March 27, 1863 – March 2, 1864
    (Maritime History Archives, Newfoundland)

George Pepperell (C20991)

19. London – Rio de Janeiro
    April 21, 1864 – December 6, 1864
    (Maritime History Archives, Newfoundland)

20. Liverpool – Pernambuco
    December 17, 1864 – April 5, 1865.
    (National Archives, BT 99/230)

21. Liverpool – Nueva Bay, Patagonia
    May 28, 1865 – November 25, 1865
    (National Archives, BT 99/230 XP 918)

22. Liverpool – Bahia
    December 13, 1865 – May 5, 1866
    (Maritime History Archives, Newfoundland)

23. Liverpool – Bahia
    June 12, 1866 – December 27, 1866
    (Maritime History Archives, Newfoundland)

24. Liverpool – Pernambuco
    February 23, 1867 – August 21, 1867
    (Maritime History Archives, Newfoundland)

25. Liverpool – Bahia
    October 18, 1867 – April 8, 1868
    (Maritime History Archives, Newfoundland)

26. Liverpool – the Brazils
    June 3, 1868 – November 19, 1868
    (Maritime History Archives, Newfoundland)

27. Liverpool – Bahia
    January 5, 1869 – July 16, 1869
    (Maritime History Archives, Newfoundland)

28. Liverpool – Bahia
    September 23, 1869 – April 9, 1870
    (Liverpool Record Office, Liverpool)

29. Liverpool – Pernambuco
    May 20, 1870 – November 4, 1870
    (Liverpool Record Office, Liverpool)

Stephen Goodman (S50983)

30. Liverpool – New Calabar
    March 16, 1871 – March 11, 1872
    (Maritime History Archives, Newfoundland)

John Campbell (S4882)

31. Liverpool – New Calabar
    May 11, 1872 – October, 1872
    (Maritime History Archives, Newfoundland)

Run from Aberdeen to Newcastle (originally to Liverpool)

and to be moored in dock (at Liverpool) and the anchors on board to the satisfaction of the Master. ... It is also agreed that advance notes will be given payable by Messrs. Alexander Hall & Co. three days after the vessel sails. The crew shall also be on board on the afternoon of the 6th inst. to bend cables and clear decks ... The voyage altered to Newcastle.

Master and Crew

Name	Age	Place of Birth	Rank	Place of Discharge/Desertion
Thomas Kemp	28	Liverpool	Master	Remains on ship
John Hylam	27	Sussex	Mate	North Shields
George M. Berth	29	Wick	Boatswain	North Shields
Joseph Twigg	53	Gravesend	Carpenter	North Shields
George Grafton	18	Inveraray	Cook	North Shields
– Thompson	32	Peterhead	Steward	North Shields
Abon Allen	27	Aberdeen	AB	North Shields
– Reid	28	Aberdeen	AB	North Shields
William Stewart	26	Aberdeen	AB	North Shields
Richard Sheldrake	30	Suffolk	AB	North Shields
William Clark	51	Montrose	AB	North Shields
William Tulloch	37	Lewick	AB	North Shields

Roderick McKenzie	59	Ross	AB	North Shields
James Sherriffs	57	Aberdeen	AB	North Shields
John Lomond	17	Dundee	OS	North Shields
John W. Kay	17	Abderdeen	OS	North Shields
Charles Brown	17	Peterhead	OS	North Shields
William Crisp	19	Yarmouth	AB	North Shields (Remains)

Voyage from North Shields to Rio de Janeiro

and any port or ports in South America wherever Freight or Trade may offer and home to her final port of discharge in the United Kingdom or the Continent of Europe. The probable length of Voyage, about Six Months.

Master and Crew

Name	Age	Place of Birth	Rank	Place of Discharge/Desertion
Thomas Kemp	28	Liverpool	Master	Bristol (Remains)
James Christie Edi	25	London	Mate	Bristol
Archibald McDougald	41	Peterhead	Boatswain	Rio de Janeiro
Joseph McBeath	31	Wick	Carpenter	Bristol
John Roberts	42	Trieste	AB	Rio de Janeiro
William Crisp	19	Teignmouth	AB	Buenos Aires
William Jones	19	Pembroke	OS	Rio de Janeiro
John Gray	24	Glasgow	AB	Rio de Janeiro
Jeremiah Cronin	24	Cork	AB	Rio de Janeiro
Thomas Reed	17	Middlesex	OS	Rio de Janeiro (Deserted)
William Campbell	19	Troon	AB	Rio de Janeiro (Deserted)
Evan Owens	23	London	AB	Bristol
John Burrows	23	Waddington	AB	Bristol

Samuel Wood	19	Dundee	OS	Rio de Janeiro
Thomas Payne	19	London	OS	Rio de Janeiro (Deserted)
Nicholas Hughes	18	Ardcolm	OS	Bristol
William Donnell	40	Trieste	AB	Rio de Janeiro
Juan Bono	20	Trieste	Steward	Rio de Janeiro
James Williams	26	Marseilles	AB	Rio de Janeiro
Frederick Roderick	30	Valparaiso	AB	Rio de Janeiro (Deserted)
Charles Jenkins	40	New Providence	Cook	Bristol

Enlisted at Rio de Janeiro

John Anderson	24	Norway	OS	Bristol
Peter Tozer	29	Devon	OS	Bristol
William Mason	29	London	AB	Bristol
Robert Wasp	35	Baltimore	AB	Bristol
John Allison	20	Troon	AB	Bristol
William Watson	21	New York	AB	Bristol
John Sully	30	New York	AB	Bristol
James Kenney	48	Liverpool	Boatswain	Bristol
T. de Lichy	28	Hamburgh	Steward	Buenos Aires
Robert Batonsky	21	Danzig	OS	Bristol
Thomas Jansen	22	Norway	OS	Bristol

Alfred Elleray	21	Manchester	OS	Bristol
Jacob Meir	24	Hamburgh	Steward	Buenos Aires (Did not board)
William Green	24	Demerera	AB	Bristol
James Thomas Wilson	21	Lancaster	Steward	Bristol

Official Log – Missing

June 8, 1854 to May 10, 1855

Voyage from Liverpool to Shanghai

Master and Crew

Name	*Rank*	*Place of discharge/desertion*
Thomas Kemp	Master	Liverpool (Remains)
John Hunter	Mate	Liverpool
George Miller	Boatswain	Liverpool
Thomas Ellesworth	Carpenter	Liverpool
Joseph Ramsay	Steward	Liverpool
William Webster	Cook	Liverpool
George Vining	–	Liverpool
John Edwards	AB/OS	Shanghai (Deserted)
John Sims	AB/OS	Shanghai (Deserted)
William Andrews	AB/OS	Hong Kong (Deserted)
Alexander Wilson	AB	Drowned
John Marley	AB/OS	Hong Kong
William Todd	AB/OS	Hong Kong
Adam Brown	AB/OS	Liverpool
John James	AB/OS	Hong Kong

Arthur Jones	AB/OS	Hong Kong
John Murphy	AB/OS	Liverpool
William Morley	AB/OS	Liverpool
Joseph Trapps	AB/OS	Hong Kong
Thomas Newry	AB/OS	Hong Kong
Thomas Bilton	AB/OS	Shanghai (Deserted)
Harry Hallett	AB/OS	Shanghai (Deserted)
Robert Parr	AB/OS	Shanghai (Deserted)

Apprentices

John Carruthers	Halifax, Nova Scotia (Deserted)
James Burns	
Edward Chaplin	

Names of additional crew

(To replace those discharged or deserted at China ports or who were discharged at Halifax.)

Name	*Place of discharge/desertion*
Albert Houkson	Liverpool
Hein Hagen	Liverpool
Andres P. Knutsen	Liverpool
Edwin Byl	Liverpool
William Roberts	Liverpool

Henry Axton	Deserted
John Tracy	Halifax
John Allan	Halifax
William Thompson	Halifax
John Ellis	Halifax
John Sheehan	Halifax
Chinaman	Liverpool
Edward Nuttell	Liverpool
Horam Manning	Liverpool
Edward Knowles	Liverpool
John Roberts	Liverpool
John Williams	Liverpool
Pedro Martin	Liverpool

Entries from the Official Log

August 21, 1854

1.30 a.m. Civil Time

At 1.30 a.m. Alexander Wilson AB fell overboard while hauling tite (sic) the Port Fore Brace, it blowing a Stormy gale at the time with heavy Sea. Their (sic) was no possible chance of saving him.

September 21,1854. Hong Kong

6 a.m. Civil Time

At 6 a.m. Adam Brown, William Todd, John James, John Marley, Thomas Newry, William Andrews all refused duty, saying that they could not work on account of the Forecastle being Leaky. At 10.45 a.m. Civil Time, Joseph Trapps refused duty and joined with the rest.

September 21, 1854. Hong Kong

Noon.

Took the seven Seamen before the Captain of the Port. They complained of the Forecastle being Leaky.

At 3 p.m.

The above men returned on board.

At 3.30 p.m.

All turned too (sic) their duty.

September 14, 1854.

9.30 a.m.

William Webster, Cook, refused duty. His plea was that two of the Crew had been beating him.

At 11 a.m. he turned to his duty.

September 23, 1854. Hong Kong

6.15 a.m.

Ordered William Webster to leave the cooking on account of the frequent complaints from the crew of their Victuals being spoiled. I am sorry to say that it has been the case with everything belonging to the Cabin since leaving Liverpool.

September 25, 1854. Hong Kong

2.15 p.m. Civil Time.

At 2.15 p.m. entered on board and found John Hunter, Chief Officer, drunk and unfit for his duty. Ordered him to his room. He remains on deck and gave me all manner of abuse. Sorry to say that it is not the first time that I have seen him in Liquor. (Co-signed by George Vining)

September 26, 1854. Hong Kong

10 a.m.

Asked John Hunter to go on Shore to see the Captain of the Port as I could not think of him remaining any longer as Chief Officer of the Mimosa. He told me that he would not leave the ship without I got a warrant for him.

September 26, 1854. Hong Kong

William Webster still refuses to do any more work. I have offered to give him whatever wages be his worth to remain on board (until) his discharge with the Sanction of the Captain of the Port.

September 27, 1854. Hong Kong

11. a.m.

Went with John Hunter to the Captain of the Port. Gave him his discharge with the consent of all parties.

Thursday, September 28, 1854. Hong Kong

2 p.m

At 2 p.m. Thomas Newry (and) Adam Brown drunk and very insolent. Ordered them to go forward and turn in. They refused doing so (and) remained aft demanding their discharge.

At 2.30 p.m. Thomas Newry went into the cabin. Would not go on deck when told. Called the assistance of the Carpenter and put a pair of handcuffs on him.

Adam Brown would not leave the quarter deck. Put a pair of handcuffs on him. When in the act of doing so John James came Aft with a Knife in his hand and called out to the rest of the people forward to come Aft and not to allow a man to be put in Irons.

At 2.45 p.m. William Andrews (and) John James refused duty.

At 4 p.m. Got assistance from the Police Station and took Thomas Newry, Adam Brown, William Andrews, John James (and) William Todd on Shore to the Police Station.

This is the second time these men have been on Shore, and the Ship has only been in Port one week. They have been doing all they could to annoy me and my officers since arriving in Hong Kong.

(Co-signed by George Vining)

September 28, 1854. Hong Kong

5 p.m.

The following five men, Thomas Newry, Adam Brown, William Andrews, John James (and) William Todd were committed to prison for the night.

Friday, September 29, 1854. Hong Kong

11 a.m.

Appeared before the Captain of the Port. Had the five men brough up before the Marine Magistrate. William Todd was willing to return on board to his duty.

Adam Brown, John James, Thomas Newry (and) William Andrews were put back untill (sic) Monday.

Friday, September 29, 1854. Hong Kong

2 p.m.

28

William Todd returned on board and turned too (sic) his duty.

Monday, October 2, 1854. Hong Kong.

11 a.m. Civil Time.

Had the four men before the Marine Magistrate. They all refused duty complaining of the Forecastle being Leaky. Adam Brown, Thomas Newry were committed to prison for one week hard labour. William Andrews being the leader amongst the men, the Magistrate committed him to prison for fourteen days hard labour. John James committed for one month for coming on the quarter deck with a Knife in his hand and calling out to the rest of the men forward to come Aft and not allow a man to be put in Irons.

October 2, 1854. Hong Kong

Gave Joseph Trapps (and) John Manley their discharge by the consent of all parties concerned, they being useless members on board the Ship.

October 9, 1854. Hong Kong

11 a.m.

Adam Brown (and) Thomas Newry refused to join the Ship. The Magistrate told them that they would be committed to prison for 84 days if they did not go on board at Noon. They consented to go on board and (to) turn to their duty again.

At 1 p.m the above men came on board and turned too (sic) their duty.

October 11, 1854. Hong Kong

William Andrews and John James refused to join the Ship. The Vessel being all ready for Sea and to proceed to Whampoo and their time in prison not expiring for several days after the ship leaves gave them their discharge with the consent of all parties.

October 23, 1854. Hong Kong

Noon.

Arthur Jones, Thomas Newry (and) William Todd being very dissatisfied and continually complaining about the forecastle, and when sent about any work always trying to do is as slow and as bad as possible. Took them to the Captain of the Port and gave them their discharge with the consent of all parties.

Monday, December 4, 1854. Shanghae

6 a.m.

Found that Harry Hallett, Thomas Bilton, Robert Parr (and) John Edwards had taken their clothes and deserted from the ship.

December 6, 1854. Shanghae

6 a.m.

Found that John Sims had taken his clothes and deserted from the Ship.

April 16, 1855. Halifax, N.S.

At 6 a.m.

Found that John Carruthers, an apprentice, has deserted from the Ship. Used all possible means to recover him, but did not succeed.

May 7, 1855. Liverpool River

About 7.30 p.m.

Found that William Manning, John Allan and Edward Knowles was (sic) absent out of the Ship, having gone on Shore without Leave when entering into the George's Basin. William Manning and John Allan got on board at 4 p.m. on the 8th May.

Voyage from Liverpool to Rio de Janeiro

Master and Crew

Name	Age	Place of Birth	Rank	Place of discharge/desertion
Thomas Kemp	36	Liverpool	Master	Liverpool (Remains)
George Miller	26	Liverpool	Mate	Liverpool
David James	32	Fishguard	Boatswain	Liverpool
Johann Christien	28	Hamburgh	Carpenter	Liverpool
John White	25	Liverpool	Sailmaker	Liverpool
Joseph Ramsay	50	Jamaica	Steward	Liverpool
Samuel Tait	35	Washington	Cook	Liverpool
John Boyle	23	Liverpool	AB	Liverpool
John Palmer	27	Sweden	AB	Liverpool
John Brown	22	Jersey	AB	Liverpool
John Rohmel	32	Sweden	AB	Liverpool
Anthony Lopez	24	Portugal	AB	Liverpool
Antonio Frank	23	Valparaiso	AB	Liverpool
Stephen Hastings	38	Stockholm	AB	Liverpool
George Moss	23	Woodbridge	AB	Liverpool

Peter Levins	21	Drogheda	OS	Liverpool
William Perry	18	Liverpool	OS	Rio de Janeiro
George Cary	17	Staffordshire	Boy	Liverpool

Apprentices

Name	Date of Indenture	Port at which Indentured
Edward Chaplin	March 30, 1854	Bristol
John Jones	June 2, 1855	Liverpool

Official Log – Missing

Voyage from Liverpool to Shanghai

thence if required to any ports and places in the China or Eastern Seas, Pacific Ocean, for wherever freight may offer, and back to a final port of discharge in the United Kingdom for a term not exceeding three years.

Master and Crew

Name	Age	Place of Birth	Rank	Place of Discharge/desertion
Thomas Kemp	36	Liverpool	Master	London (Remains)
Matthew Afleck	23	Dumfries	Mate	London (Remains)
George Irvine	23	Worthington	Boatswain	London
John Christian	29	Hamburg	Carpenter	London
John Kerr	25	Belfast	Boatswain	London
Samuel Tate	36	Washington	Steward	London
Charles Jones	28	Washington	Cook	Shanghai (Deserted)
Frank Ross	29	Belfast	AB	London
Henry Du Bass	21	Lyons	AB	Shanghai
John Olive	26	France	AB	Shanghai
Alex Lowe	21	Bristol	AB	London
Ion McCarthy	26	Scotland	AB	London
Charles Debassé	26	Antwerp	AB	London

John Bergen	28	Hamberg	AB	London
George Wolfe	39	Copenhagen	AB	London
William Henderson	26	Liverpool	AB	London
William –	28	Amsterdam	AB	London
M. Hookstan	29	Amsterdam	AB	London
(Name illegible)	38	New York	AB	London

Apprentices

Name	Age	Date of Indenture	Port of Indenture
George Harvey Carey	18	12 February, 1856	Liverpool
James Burns	16	7 February, 1856	Liverpool
John Jones	16	2 March, 1855	Liverpool
Edward Chaplin	17	30 March, 1854	Liverpool

Official Log – Missing

Run from London to Liverpool

Master and Crew

Name	Age	Place of Birth	Rank	Place of discharge/desertion
Thomas Kemp	36	Liverpool	Master	Liverpool (Remains)
Matthew Affleck	24	Dumfries	Mate	Liverpool
George Irving	24	Whitehaven	Boatswain	Liverpool
John Mayne	36	Woolwich	Cook/Steward	Liverpool
William Anderson	45	London	AB	Liverpool
William Bollard	38	Richmond	AB	Liverpool
William Brink	49	Bingham	AB	Liverpool
Charles Granger	45	London	AB	Liverpool
William Seath	35	Essex	AB	Liverpool
William Goodman	33	London	AB	Liverpool
Frederick Hines	29	Yarmouth	AB	Liverpool
Philip Cotter	44	London	AB	Liverpool
James Wallis	25	Plymouth	AB	Liverpool
William Major	28	London	AB	Liverpool

Apprentices

Name	Age	Place of Birth	Date of Indenture	Port of Indenture
Edward Chaplin	18	Southampton	30 March, 1854	Bristol
George Henry Carey	17	Fenton	12 July, 1856	Liverpool
James Burns	16	Glasgow	12 July, 1856	Liverpool
John Jones	15	Liverpool	2 January, 1855	Liverpool

Official Log – Missing

Voyage from Liverpool to Rio de Janeiro

Master and Crew

Name	Age	Place of Birth	Rank	Place of discharge/desertion
Thomas Kemp	34	Liverpool	Master	Liverpool
Matthew Affleck	21	Ayr	Mate	Liverpool
John Christian	30	Hamburg	Carpenter	Liverpool
James Ward	21	Hull	Boatswain	Rio de Janeiro
John White	26	Liverpool	Sailmaker	Liverpool
William Stacey	21	Bridgewater	Steward	Liverpool
John Powell	35	Bideford	Cook	Liverpool
Joseph Tucker	30	Liverpool	AB	Liverpool
George Howard	33	Baltimore	AB	Rio de Janeiro (Deserted)
Francis Murray	21	Dundee	AB	Liverpool
William Wilson	42	Liverpool	AB	Did not board
James Walker	30	Leith	AB	Liverpool
William Cornelius	24	Deal	AB	Liverpool
William Lamb	22	Liverpool	AB	Liverpool
Matthew Lamb	24	Guernsey	AB	Liverpool

Thomas Palmer	24	Cheshire	AB	Liverpool
Thomas Taylor	43	Liverpool	AB	Liverpool

Enlisted at Rio de Janeiro

Frank –	18	Oxford	AB	Liverpool
George McGuire	19	America	AB	Mauritius (Deserted)

Apprentices

Name	Date of Indenture	Port of Indenture
Edward Chaplin	March 30, 1854	Bristol
George Harvey Carey	July 1, 1856	Liverpool
John Jones	June 2, 1853	Liverpool

Official log – Missing

Voyage from Liverpool to Rio de Janeiro

thence, if required, to any ports and places in South America and the Pacific, Indian and Atlantic Oceans, thence to a port for orders, and to the Continent (if required) and back to a final port of discharge in the United Kingdom, the term not to exceed two years.

Master and Crew

Name	Age	Place of Birth	Rank	Place of discharge/desertion
Trevanion Hugo	34	Devonshire	Master	Liverpool (Remains)
John Furniss	25	Manchester	Mate	Liverpool
Alexander Stevenson	29	–	Carpenter	Liverpool
Robert Smith	32	Ayr	Boatswain	Liverpool
Daniel Hyde Lloyd	22	Liverpool	Steward	Liverpool
James Gough	28	Drogheda	Cook	Rio de Janeiro (Died)
Laurente Notson	23	Sweden	Sailmaker	Liverpool
John Fagrell	22	Sweden	AB	Liverpool
Wm. Henry Miller	29	Penzance	AB	Liverpool
Eric Silein	32	Stockholm	AB	Liverpool
Thomas Morris	28	Deal	AB	Liverpool
Matthew Shamrock	22	St. Mawes	AB	Did not board

Name	Age		Rating	
Benjamin Bowden	24	–	AB	Liverpool
John Boyce	23	Lowestoft	AB	Liverpool
John Francis	20	Manchester	Boy	Liverpool
Neil McKey	20	Arran	AB	Rio de Janeiro (Died)

Enlisted at Rio de Janeiro

William Bridgwater	26	Richmond	OS	Liverpool
Charles Anderson	35	Philadelphia	Cook	Liverpool

Apprentices

Name	Date of Indenture	Place of Indenture
Edward Chaplin	March 30, 1854	Bristol
James Burns	July 7, 1856	Liverpool
Bancroft Stringer	April 20, 1857	Liverpool

Entries from the Official Log

November 23, 1857. St. George's Channel

John Boyce (Seaman) creating a disturbance about stowing the Mainsail. Being asked by the Master what was the matter Boyce became insolent, saying he be Bg.d. if he wouldn't leave the Ship in Rio the first chance. For his insolence I exact full penalty.

December 8, 1857

7 a.m.

Came on Deck about 7. Looking Foreward I saw John Boyce strike Eric Silein in the face. I asked the reason afterwards why he done so. He said because Silein hosed a bucket of water over him. The Boatswain standing (by) said he did not see anything of the kind. I find (sic) him full penalty which the law exacts for this offence.

December 12, 1857

About 6.30 p.m.

Going Foreward saw the yards wanted trimming. Mate called the watch, but no movement. Told the mate for the future to have one Watch on Deck. With that, John Boyce interfered saying it was time they had tea. Long before this he came out of the Forecastle to me in a threatening and insolent manner, he having had then three quarters of an hour to tea and his Watch on Deck. He also became abusive, defying me. I told him I would punish him some other time. I also find (sic) him full penalty of the Law.

December 29, 1857. Rio de Janeiro Harbour

While mooring the Vessel heard a noise Foreward. Went foreward to see what was the matter. John Boyce, Seaman, being very annoying to the Mate causeing (sic) a delay in the work was spoken to by the Mate about his conduct. Challenged the Mate out to fight in my presence. This man has carried on (in) a mutinous spirit ever since leaving Liverpool.

January 30, 1858. Rio de Janeiro

Neil McKey, Seaman, sent to the hospital with Yellow Fever. Died on the 4th day of February as certified by the British Consul in the back of the Articles. His effects were taken in the Cabin and were sold by Public Auction.

February 6, 1858. Rio de Janeiro

James Gough, Cook, sent to the hospital with Yellow Fever. Died on the 16th as certified on the Articles by the British Consul.

March 4, 1858. On leaving Rio de Janeiro

About 7 a.m.

Charles Anderson who shipped as Cook at Rio de Janeiro came on board on the 4th at about 7 a.m. being the worse for drink. Went Foreward and laid down untill (sic) evening. He turned too (sic) in the Galley in a short time. Soon found (that) he knew very little about cooking. Tried him for 3 or 4 days, but could make no good of him. I was obliged to put another man in and turn him out as the people were complaining that he was spoiling their food. He has since been doing duty about Deck as Ordinary Seaman although not able to steer.

April 14, 1858. Paraíba

About 7.30 p.m.

Being on shore at that time saw M.H.Miller and Thomas Morris, Seamen. I asked the reason why they were on shore contrary to my orders. Miller made answer that they had a right to come on shore after 6 o'clock when they thought proper. I ordered them on board the vessel which they did not do untill (sic) next morning. For disobedience of orders I exact full penalty of the law.

Tuesday, April 13, 1858. Paraíba

Benjamin Bowden and John Fagrell, Seamen, after being on shore a few hours on liberty were taken up by the Brazilian authorities and put in jail for being drunk and disorderly in the streets and did not return on board untill (sic) April 15th in charge of two soldiers as certified on the back of the Articles by the British Consul.

April 21, 1858. Paraíba

Requiring all the crew to work the vessel took Charles Anderson back to the Galley again. The first day or two done his work very well. On the 22nd spoilt all the pea soup, the crew having to go without. I also told him about cleaning the mess lids which was in a filthy state, he being too lazy to clean them.

April 28, 1858. At Sea

Cook had orders to get breakfast ready at 8, but was not ready till twenty five minutes to 9. I can get nothing but insolence and contemptuous looks from this man. The crew has also made complaint about the filthy state the meat is cooked (in). I saw myself 4 lbs. of meat cut off one piece of beef not fit to eat. For this incompetence of duty I shall exact full penalty of the law.

May 1, 1858

Have been obliged this day to turn Charles Anderson, Cook, out of the galley, not being able to cook the food given to him, also for his filthiness which was not fit for anyone to eat, after the crew also making complaint that they had got no tea, it being then seven o'clock p.m. Have put another man in to do his work. I therefore reduce his wages to Ordinary Seaman pay £3 per month from the time of his being turned out of the galley after leaving Rio de Janeiro for not being able to perform for what he shipped for.

Voyage from Liverpool to Rio de Janeiro

Master and Crew

Name	Age	Place of Birth	Rank	Place of discharge/desertion
Trevanion Hugo	34	Devonshire	Master	Liverpool (Remains)
William Patrick Morgan	25	Norway	Mate	Liverpool
James Smith	36	Orkney	Carpenter	Liverpool
Robert Smith	32	Ayr	Boatswain	Liverpool
Thos.Lawrence Colkis	36	Stanley Bridge	Steward	Rio de Janeiro (Deserted)
William Catley	30	Milford	Cook	Liverpool
Lawrence Knutson	25	Sweden	AB	Liverpool
James Randall	37	Sydney	AB	Liverpool
John Peterson	24	Sweden	AB	Liverpool
James Hearn	22	Dundee	AB	Liverpool
John Wilson	26	Sweden	AB	Liverpool
Thomas Lewis	35	Aberystwyth	AB	Liverpool
Isaac Smith	24	Devonshire	AB	Liverpool
James Howard	23	Dublin	AB	Liverpool
John Edward Davis	20	Manchester	OS	Liverpool
William Simons	19	Bristol	OS	Liverpool

Apprentices

Name	Date of Indenture	Port of Indenture
Bancroft Stringer	20 April, 1857	Liverpool
Edward Chaplin	30 March, 1854	Bristol
James Burns	7 February, 1856	Liverpool

Official Log – Missing

Voyage from Liverpool to Rio de Janeiro

Master and Crew

Name	Age	Place of Birth	Rank	Place of discharge/desertion
Trevanion Hugo	35	Devonshire	Master	Liverpool (Remains)
George Stoneman	31	Yarmouth	Mate	Liverpool
Robert Smith	32	Ayr	Boatswain	Liverpool
James Smith	36	Scotland	Carpenter	Liverpool
John Graham	22	Alexandria	Steward	Did not board
William Cately	30	Milford	Cook	Liverpool
Henry Barnsley	21	Wisbeach	AB	Rio de Janeiro
Samuel Reid	30	Liverpool	AB	Rio de Janeiro (Died)
John Nelson	22	Leith	AB	Liverpool
Thomas Smith	21	Glasgow	AB	Rio de Janeiro (Died)
David Davis	24	Sweden	AB	Liverpool
Alfred Evans	27	Cardigan	AB	Liverpool
James Evans	22	Cardigan	AB	Did not board
Edward Stanley	22	St. John, N.B.	AB	Liverpool
James Davies	18	London	AB	Rio de Janeiro

Robert Leslie	32	Jamaica	Steward	Liverpool
Peter Nash	20	Sweden	AB	Liverpool

Enlisted at Rio de Janeiro

Henry Hodges	32	Plymouth	AB	Liverpool
John Doyle	22	Dublin	AB	Liverpool
Abraham Longdon	34	Manchester	Deckhand	Died at sea
John Devitt	–	Lettercarney	OS	Liverpool
John Locket	13	Scotland	Boy	Liverpool

Entries from the Official Log

February 28, 1859. At Sea

Henry Barnsley off duty sick with Venereal Disease. Not being able to perform his duty on account of his having an intense swelling in the Groin. Treated him as directed in Medical Book for Buboes.

March 17, 1859

Henry Barnsley better. Turned to work still being sick.

April 29, 1859

In Rio de Janeiro Henry Barnsley complained of getting worse and wished to go to the Hospital and was sent to the

Misercordia by an order from the Consulate.

July 10, 1859

9 a.m.

This day John Doyle being Employed to take down Rigging with a Caution not to let any of the tar fall on the paint to destroy it. Contrary to orders he let some come down on Deck and on the paint. Myself standing by, I received some on my Coat. Being told about it he insisted that he did not let it come down although I saw it myself and making lie to my face. I told him (that) I would punish him in Liverpool for this and (that) his former Conduct (would be) entered herein. He laughed at me and told me he did care a Dam (sic) for that. Considers he has a right to spoil and destroy the paint of the Vessel, and being spoke to rather sharp about it (he says that) I am bullying him and gives me insolence in return. I shall therefore put this and other entries in the hands of the Board of Trade to inflict what penalty they may think proper to enforce for this Conduct while on board this Vessel.

October 26, 1859 to April 25, 1860

Voyage from Liverpool to Rio de Janeiro

thence (if required) to any ports and places in South America, thence to a port for orders and to the Continent of Europe (if required) and back to a given port of discharge in the United Kingdom, the voyage not to exceed twelve months.

Master and Crew

Name	Age	Place of Birth	Rank	Place of discharge/desertion
Trevanion Hugo	35	Devonshire	Master	Liverpool (Remains)
George Stoneman	34	Yarmouth	Mate	Liverpool
James Smith	33	Scotland	Carpenter	Liverpool
Robert Smith	33	Ayr	Boatswain	Liverpool
James Randall	38	Sydney, Nova Scotia	Sailmaker	Liverpool
George Mitchell	26	Glasgow	Steward	Did not board
David Howell	39	Liverpool	Cook	Rio de Janeiro (Deserted)
Charles Brown	25	Hampshire	AB	Liverpool
William Remison	39	Deptford	AB	Liverpool
William Allen	22	Dundee	AB	Liverpool
Charles Berg	37	Sweden	AB	Liverpool
Alexander McJames	23	Glasgow	AB	Liverpool
James Vaughan	22	Liverpool	AB	Rio de Janeiro (Deserted)

Alfred Mills	22	Liverpool	AB	Liverpool
Walter Evans	15	Chester	Boy	Liverpool
Evan Davies	17	Aberystwyth	OS	Liverpool
James Knight	17	Gloucester	OS	Liverpool

Enlisted at Rio de Janeiro

William Dubarry	45	Demerera	Steward	Liverpool
Thomas Murray	30	Jamaica	Cook	Liverpool
Thomas Dodd	19	Dover	AB	Liverpool

Apprentices

Name	*Date of Indenture*	*Port of Indenture*
John Jones	June 2, 1855	Liverpool

Entries from the Official Log

October 28, 1858. Salthouse Dock, Liverpool

Ship Mimosa being ready for Sea, but prevented by contrary winds.

October 29, 1859

Ship Mimosa lying in the Salthouse Dock ready for Sea did not proceed to Sea, it being detained on account of the Weather.

The names inserted (below) did not come on board to their duty as directed in the Articles this 29th day of October, 1859.

James Smith, Carpenter

Robert Smith, Boatswain

James Randall, Sailmaker

Charles Brown, Seaman

David Howell, Cook

William Remison, Seaman

William Allen, Seaman

Charles Berg, Seaman

Alexander McJames, Seaman

James Vaughan, Seaman

Alfred Mills, Seaman

Walter Evans, Ordinary Seaman

James Knight, Ordinary Seaman

Evan Davis, Ordinary Seaman

Monday, October 31, 1859

Wind fresh from SW. Ship Mimosa hauled out of Dock into the River. The crew came on board at the Pier Head and turned to work, with the exception of George Mitchell who Deserted. Shipped William Dubarry as substitute. Charles Berg came on board intoxicated and did not do any dury until Wednesday, November the 2nd.

November 6, 1859. Off Point Lynas

Blowing very hard at the time requiring all hands to man the ship round. All hands at their stations but Charles Berg and Charles Brown, Seamen. Going Forward to see why they did not come Aft when called (and) said they was not able. I asked them why, but (they) could not give me any satisfactory answer. I insisted uppon (sic) their going Aft. Brown not very willing to do so. I gave him a push. With that Brown squared up to fight me, but the 2nd Mate stoped (sic) the Blow and he was put on his back. He got up the 2nd time and squared up to fight. I was obliged to strike him or receive the Blow. He went on with his duty very well after that. Before this occurrence he showed signs of a Mutinous Conduct to me and my officers.

November 12, 1859. Off Cape Clear

William Dubarry who shipped as Steward in the Room (place of) of George Mitchell (who) deserted as substitute. I soon found that he was no Steward and could not get the requisite meals ready, was also very dirty, that he was not fit to be in a Cabin. I therefore turned him out of the Cabin for being impertinent as a Steward, but also for Filthiness.

November 13, 1859

Complaints haveing (sic) been made by the Crew about David Howell, Cook, as to the manner (that) their food was cooked and the filthy state (that) everything was cooked in, I went Foreward and examined (for) myself and found everything as was represented and having previously warned him about it, I could not put up with it any longer. I turned him out of the Galley and put William Dubarry in as Cook to see how he could manage there. David Howell is doing duty now as an Ordinary Seaman. Being a Disabled man, (he) cannot go aloft. I shall reduce his Wages to that as an Ordinary Seaman.

November 15, 1859

Have this day been obliged to turn William Dubarry out of the Galley not being able to cook and for making away with part of a Fowl sent to get cooked and put David Howell back again to do the best (he can). William Dubarry is doing duty about deck as Deck Hand. I therefore shall reduce his Wages one half for shipping for a Duty which he is not able to perform.

Sunday, November 27, 1859

At 1 p.m.

Part of the Crew brought their Pudding Aft for me to see which they had to Eat, and I must say I never saw such stuff in my life. It was not fit for a Pig to make use, although I make use of the same flour at my table. I have been obliged to issue a Second Compliment of Flour for the Men to get cooked for themselves as best they could. This is not the first or second time I have had this complaint from the Crew, and not without cause. I shall therefore leave the case in the hands of the Board of Trade to consider what penalty to be inflicted uppon (sic) such a Man as calls himself a Cook. His whole arrangements are dirty.

Thursday, November 24, 1859

About noon.

I have this day taken Alexander McJames, Seaman, to do his Duty as Steward in the Cabbin (sic) in the Room of William Dubarry and I therefore agree to pay him at the same Wages as Dubarry, now turned out of the cabbin, as long as he continues to do the duty as Steward of the said Vessel, Viz. three pounds per month.

January 7, 1860. Rio de Janeiro

James Vaughan, Seaman, being ill with dysentery was sent to the Hospital on the 14th. Was sent out quite well, but he never returned to the Vessel. Reported him at the British Consul, but could not find him. Shipped another man in his Room, but had to pay higher wages, also a police officer to find him at $4,000 Milreis per day. He had left his Effects. Sold at Auction.

	£	s	d
Lot 1. 1 Gunneysack, 2 Singlets, 1 Vest, 1 Cotton Shirt		3	0
Lot 2. 1 Cotton Shirt, 1 Vest, 1 Drawers, 1 Jumper		3	0
Lot 3. 1 Shirt, 1 Vest, 1 Drawers, 1 Trousers, 1 Jumper		5	0
Lot 4. 2 Flannel Shirts,		4	9
Lot 5. 1 Jacket, 2 prs. Stockings, Comforter		5	6
Lot 6. 2 Flannel Shirts, 1 Handkerchiefs		2	6
Lot 7. 1 pr. Blankets		6	0
Total Amount:	1	9	9

Friday, January 13, 1860. Rio de Janeiro

At 4 p.m.

Alfred Mills, Seaman, being aloft bending sails was idleing (sic) away his time was spoke to by me, the Master, to get on with his work. Mills made some saucy answer. I told him (that) if he gave me any more of it I would punish him. He said (that) it was more than I could do. I told him (that) he had better come down and try. He did so and stood out to fight. After Mills getting the worst of it returned to his work as before a much better Man.

January 18, 1860. Rio de Janeiro

David Howell who shipped as Cook at Liverpool was duly discharged at Rio de Janeiro and Wages (were) paid him before the British Consul as inserted on the back of the Articles.

Thursday, February 8, 1860

This entry is made against Thomas Murray who shipped as Cook at Rio (de) Janeiro. After leaving port found that Murray was no Cook. In the way which the food was sent to the table could not make use of it and have been obliged to throw it away and also the Complaints from the Crew about the manner (in which) their food was cooked. I reasoned with the Cook at first and told him to try and mend (his ways), but I found reasoning no use. I was obliged to use harsh words, but to my surprise I found (him) an insolent dirty fellow. His person is filthy, also (the) Galley and everything belonging to it. When spoken to by me, the Master, I am treated with Contempt and Insolence and also defyes (sic) me to do anything with him. This man has aggravated me to that degree on purpose to strike him so has (sic) to get a pull uppon (sic) me, but I will leave the Board of Trade to settle this matter or some Magistrate.

Thursday, March 1, 1860. Harbour at Maranhao

6 p.m.

This day a Lighter of Cotton came along side of Vessel to be taken on board or pay double Lighter. At about 6 p.m. about 30 bales remaining in the Lighter. Charles Brown, William Remison, William Allen, Charles Berg and Alfred Mills, Seamen, came Aft in a body and said they would not take any more Cotton on board without (unless) I would enter into an arrangement to give them time the next day. However, I refused to enter into any arrangement, but told them I would do what was right. I asked them all personly (sic) if they would get the Cotton on board, but all made excuse saying they were tired. The above names have been sent forward and the remainder on board of the Crew still continued their duty but was obliged to stop work on account of those men refuseing (sic) duty causeing (sic) extra Literage and endangering the Cargo lying alongside the Vessel. The Ring Leader (sic) in this affair is Charles Brown who has been so from the commencement of the Voyage, as will be seen by other Entries in this Log Book.

March 17, 1860. Port of Maranhao

About 4 p.m.

This entry is made against William Allen and Charle Berg, Seamen, being sent on Shore with others of the crew to load a Lighter of Cotton and absented themselves without Leave and returned on (the) boat on Monday March the 17th to their duty. Particulars are inserted on the back of the Articles by the British Consul who had charged 5 shillings for Expenses.

March 25, 1860

This entry is against Thomas Murray, Cook, for disobedience of orders. After personaly (sic) telling him not to send any more Slush mixed with my food he still persists in doing it and when spoken to by me I get nothing but some provoking answer to annoy me, and the food is so badly cooked often times cannot make use wich (sic) I can testify by my officers.

March 26, 1860

About 1.30 p.m.

Being informed that Thomas Murray, Cook, would not give the men Slush from the Coppers for Ship's use, I went foreward and asked him why he did not give the men Slush to work with. He said in a most insolent manner (that) he had none. I went into the Galley and found a tin and handed it out. He had previous to that thrown some into some stinking black stuff. Because it should not be used for the Ship I ordered (it) to be thrown overboard, being in a putrified state. I asked Murray what he meant by not supplying the ship with Slush, he haveing (sic) no right to it. He made some very insolent reply that he would sooner throw it overboard, useing (sic) such provokeing (sic) Language and Gross Insolence. I was obliged to turn him out of the Galley and put in a Boy to do his work for I never received such insulting Language from any man before provoking me to commit myself so as to get a pull on me in Liverpool, as he says. Murray is now doing duty on deck as Ordinary Seaman and shall pay him his Wages accordingly from this date.

June 16, 1860 to January 29, 1861

Voyage from Liverpool to Rio de Janeiro and Mauritius

thence (if required) to any ports and places in the Atlantic and Pacific Oceans, thence to a port for orders to the Continent of Europe (if required) and back to a final port of discharge in the United Kingdom, the term not to exceed twelve months.

Master and Crew

Name	Age	Place of Birth	Rank	Place of discharge/desertion
Trevanion Hugo	36	Devon	Master	Liverpool (Remains)
George Stoneman	34	Yarmouth	Mate	Port Louis, Mauritius
David Bell	23	Ayr	Carpenter	Bristol
Robert Smith	32	Ayr	Boatswain	Bristol
Joseph Saunders	41	Whitehaven	Steward	Rio de Janeiro
James Howe	48	Edinburgh	Cook	Rio de Janeiro
Antonio Mane	25	Portugal	AB	Bristol
Peter Head	23	Austria	AB	Bristol
John Thompson	36	Dumfries	AB	Rio de Janeiro
Joseph Shields	30	Barbadoes	AB	Rio de Janeiro
Robert Smith	46	Margate	AB	Rio de Janeiro
Thomas Shaw	22	Belfast	AB	Rio de Janeiro
Robert Hannan	20	Belfast	AB	Rio de Janeiro

James Randall	39	Sydney, N. S.	Sailmaker	Died at sea.
John Musson	20	Liverpool	OS	Bristol
John Bloom	19	Lancashire	OS	Bristol
William John May	18	Guernsey	OS	Bristol
Maurice Coffey	16	Drogheda	Boy	Bristol

Enlisted at Rio de Janeiro

John Cluney	34	Wexford	Cook	Bristol
John Donovan	24	London	AB	Bristol
John Williams	30	London	AB	Bristol
Jasper Westfall	25	Pennsylvania	AB	Liverpool
William Campbell	36	Glasgow	AB	Liverpool
John Freytag	25	Hamburg	AB	Port Louis
William Burney	23	Berkshire	Steward	Port Louis
Charles Ord	17	Liverpool	OS	Liverpool

Enlisted at Port Louis, Mauritius

James Collins	29	Shields	AB	Bristol
L. McGee	23	Scotland	AB	Bristol
Daniel Morgan	23	Limerick	AB	Port Louis (Deserted)
Edward Thompson	21	Boston, G.B.	AB	Bristol

Entries from the Official Log

January 13, 1860. Princes Dock, Liverpool

Moderate breezes from the South. Vessel getting ready for Sea.

January 16, 1860. Liverpool

Light winds from the South. Hauled the Vessel out of Dock. The Crew all came on board the Vessel sober. The Vessel then proceeded to Sea.

June 17, 1860. Off Holly Head

Peter Head who shipped as Able Seaman was this day sent to the Wheel to steer. Was obliged to send him away. Found he could not steer at all. We also find him incompetent as Able Seaman, not being able to do Ordinary Seaman's work. I shall therefore reduce his Wages to that of an Ordinary Seaman, 30 shillings per Month.

June 17, 1860. Off Holly Head

William John May who shipped as Ordinary Seaman, found he could not steer the Vessel or do the simplest thing about the Ship, not even find a rope or know the name of one. I therefore reduce his Wages to 30 shillings per Month.

June 28, 1860

About 11.30 a.m.

Robert Smith, Seaman, being at the Helm and steering SWGW, he did not keep the Vessel on that course. Was told by the Master to keep the Vessel SWGW. He immediately put the Helm about and steered the Vessel SWGS to annoy the Master.

I shall find (sic) him two days pay for willful (sic) Disobedience of orders and turned him away from the Wheel for he was not disposed to steer the Vessel, only what way he thought proper.

July 11, 1860

About 10 a.m.

This entry is against Robert Smith for continued Disobedience and Insolence. Being aloft at work was told by the 2nd officer to come down. He did not seem inclined to do so untill (sic) insisted uppon (sic) by the Master. He gave such Abuse and Insolence (that) I was obliged to have him sent Foreward to clean (word missing) from rust. This kind of Conduct entitles him to imprisonment.

August 25, 1860. Rio de Janeiro Harbour

This entry is against Joseph Sanders, Steward, for Refusal of Duty. Being ordered by the Master to go Aft and get the tea he refused to do it. He has taken this step to get clear of the Vessel for former Conduct which I had looked over, he having consumed 5 doz. of Beer and Porter besides a quantity of Spirits. He has been turned out of the Cabbin (sic) for Disobedience and took (taken) back again, but I still find he get Drink by some means or other.

September 6, 1860. Rio de Janeiro

I have this day mustered all Hands of the ship and informed them that instead of proceeding round the Cape Horn as I intended that I intend to proceed to Port Louis in Mauritius and all those that intend to perform the Voyage in the Vessel will remain where they are. All those that do not will stand on one side and I will take them by boat to the British Consul.

September 23, 1860

About 3 p.m.

This entry is against John Donovan, Seaman. Came on deck about 3 a.m. I saw Donovan idleing (sic) his time spinning yarns with the Cook. Was ordered Aft to get on with his work by the Master. He very reluctantly did so but with a great deal of Abuse and Insolence. I told him to stop his tongue. He said he would not for me or for any other man in the Ship. I told (him) if he did not stop I would punish him. He got up from his seat and stood out and squared to fight me, the Master, provoking me to strip. However I did not think fit to put myself uppon (sic) equal footing with (the) blackguard. I will punish (him) another way.

For the first offence (of) insolence, 2 days pay. For provoking me to strike him and standing out I shall leave to the discretion of the court.

September 29, 1860. Port Louis, Mauritius

This entry is against William Burney, Steward. Came on board about 5 o'clock. Found the Steward Drunk. After examining the Lockers found one of them had been opened and some Wiskey (sic) taken out and carried (to) the pantry and found a glass with Wiskey in it. This man got Drunk in Rio de Janeiro. From that time he has not had charge of the Spirits and has continued by some means to open the Lockers wich (sic) are kept locked. I have turned him out of the Cabbin (sic) for Drunkenness and Dirtiness. He is now doing Duty on Deck as an Ordinary Seaman.

November 1, 1860. Port Louis, Mauritius

Having discharged Mr. Stoneman, Mate, this day I have appointed Robert Smith, Boatswain as Chief Mate from this port to England and his Wages to be £5 per month from this 1st day of November, 1860.

November 1, 1860

I have also appointed John Bloom to act as 2nd Officer from this 1st. day of November, 1860 from this port to England and he to be renumerated accordingly as the Master may think fit.

November 10, 1860

About noon.

This entry is made against David Bell, Carpenter, for Gross Insolence and Profane Language made use of to the Master on the Quarter Deck while at his duty. He was ordered off the Poop (deck) and refused to go. Was pushed off by me, the Master. Attempted to come up again and was pushed off a second time and told him if he attempted again I would Knock him down. He said it was just what he wanted for me to strike him, aggravating me almost to do it. For Gross Insolence, 2 days pay.

November 11, 1860. Port Louis, Mauritius

About 2 p.m.

This entry is against Daniel Morgan who shipped on board as an Able Seaman and came on board on the 9th. On the 11th was sent in the boat to put the Master on shore and ordered back to the Ship. When about half way over to the Vessel he returned to the Shore in the boat and I have not seen anything of him from the 11th up to this 14th day of November and I now (consider) him as a Deserter.

November 14, 1860. Port Louis

Daniel Morgan reported as deserted on the 11th instant not yet returned to the Ship which is nearly ready for sea. We duly declare him a Deserter.

November 23, 1860.

About 6.30 p.m.

James Randall died this day after a long illness of Disease of the Heart, haveing (sic) complained for a long time has done but very little duty for 2 Months. On arriving at the (port in) Mauritius was sent to the Hospital on the 27th day of October and returned to the Ship on the 13th of November and to his duty on the 15th. On the 16th not well, so off duty. Continued to get worse up to the 23rd when he died. His body (was committed) to the Deep. His effects are as follows:

1 Chest containing:	1 Ditty Bag (containing):
3 prs. Flannel Drawers	1 Clasp Knife and Sheath
4 Singlets	1 Razor and Strap
4 Blue Serge Shirts	1 Box Sundries
2 prs. Cloth Trousers	2 Books
4 prs. Canvas Trousers	1 yard Blue Serge
2 prs. Moleskin Trousers	1 Glengarry Cap
2 Canvas Jumpers	1 Clothes Bag
1 Cotton Striped Shirt	1 Felt Hat

6 prs. Stockings	1 Blanket	
1 Comforter	1 Rug	
1 pr. Braces	1 Monkey Jacket	
5 Handkerchiefs	Bed and Pillow thrown out	
3 Towels		

Wages Account from the 16th June to the 23rd November

5 months and 8 days	£14	9	8
Advance	2	15	0
Allotment	8	5	0
Tobacco and Cash	1	0	0
Shipping		1	0
	12	1	0
Balance	2	8	8

December 1, 1860

I have also appointed John Bloom to act as 2nd Mate from this lst day of November, 1860 from this port to England and to be renumerated accordingly as the Master may think fit.

December 11, 1860

About 7 p.m.

Against David Bell, Carpenter. Came on deck (at) about 7 and Requiring the Carpenter he was not to be found. On going Foreward found him in the Forecastle with the Crew. I asked him what he was doing there. Not giving me a satisfactory answer I told him he had better take his clothes and live there altogether, which he did haveing (sic) been previously spoken to by me for the very same thing, being so much with the Crew. It is not usual for Carpenters to mix with the Crew. He is considered as a Petty Officer, only for some conspiring purpose which I firmly believe and by the Insulting Manner (he spoke) to me and my Officers. I told him about it. He says he forgot.

December 23, 1860

About 10.30 a.m.

It was reported to me by the Boatswain that the Main Topsail yard was broken. I found it so bad (that I) was obliged to send it down. Immediately since leaving Mauritius I found out (that) the Topsail Yard was broken that morning, the Mate and David Bell, Carpenter, being present at the sceen (sic). He (the Mate) did not report the same to me which is his duty to do so, knowing the same to be broken and might have indeed (had serious) Consequences had not the Boatswain panicstrickenly found it out. I asked why he did not report it to me. He said he was afraid the Mate would give him a thrashing. This act also shows a Conspiracy with the Chief Mate who I have discharged in Mauritius.

January 28, 1861. Bristol

Moored the Mimosa in Dock at 1 p.m. when the Crew left, thus ending the Voyage.

Run from Bristol to Liverpool

and to moor the ship properly in Dock.

Master and Crew

Name	Age	Place of Birth	Rank	Place of discharge/desertion
Trevanion Hugo	36	Plymouth	Master	Liverpool (Remains)
George Poole	44	Minehead	Mate	Liverpool
Robert Smith	34	Ayr	Boatswain	Liverpool
Henry Hall	28	Bristol	Steward	Liverpool
Samuel Guffy	40	Bristol	Cook/AB	Liverpool
George Herbert	40	Bristol	AB	Liverpool
James Hippitt	39	Bristol	AB	Liverpool
James Collins	49	Bristol	AB	Liverpool
John Gazard	37	Bristol	AB	Liverpool
John Luce	53	Pill	AB	Liverpool
James Lewis	55	–	AB	Liverpool
James McGee	23	Scotland	AB	Liverpool
Antonio Maneo	25	Portugal	AB	Liverpool
Henry Thomas	29	Bristol	AB	Liverpool

| Robert Clark | 52 | Berkely | AB | Liverpool |
| Benjamin Mace | 28 | London | AB | Liverpool |

Official Log – Missing

Voyage from Liverpool to Mauritius

then (if required) to any ports and places in the Indian, Pacific and Atlantic Oceans and thence to a port for orders, and to the Continent of Europe (if required) and back to a final port of discharge in the United Kingdom. The term not to exceed two years.

Master and Crew

Name	Age	Place of Birth	Rank	Place of discharge/desertion
Trevanion Hugo	37	Devon	Master	Liverpool (Remains)
George Poole	45	Bristol	Mate	Liverpool
William Hart	29	Scarborough	Carpenter	Liverpool
Robert Smith	33	Ayr	Boatswain	Liverpool
Benjamin Stack	26	Devon	Steward	Liverpool
William Catley	32	Milford	Cook	Liverpool
Thomas Hogan	28	Queenstown	AB	Liverpool
John Bryant	25	Sweden	AB	Liverpool
Robert Lloyd	27	Brixham	AB	Port Louis
Henry Becker	33	Sweden	AB	Liverpool
Robert Johnson	36	Belfast	AB	Liverpool

Edward Hutter	24	Prussia	AB	Liverpool
William Maxted	21	Whitstable	AB	Liverpool
Robert Morgan	35	Glasgow	AB	Liverpool
Alexander Wilkie	20	Picton	OS	Liverpool
Richard Ashcroft	22	Liverpool	OS	Port Louis
John Grier	17	Dungannon	Boy	Liverpool

Enlisted at Port Louis

| Joseph Francis | 21 | Oporto | AB | Liverpool |
| G.A. Carr | 29 | Shields | AB | Liverpool |

Apprentices

Name	*Date of Indenture*	*Port of Indenture*
William Tisdale	January 19, 1861	Liverpool
John Longshaw	March 21, 1861	Liverpool

Entries from the Official Log

March 30, 1861. Princes Dock, Liverpool

Hauled the Vessel to the Dock gates, but did not proceed to Sea on account of the weather.

March 31, 1861

About 1 p.m.

Hauled the Vessel out of dock. The Crew all came on board at the Pier Head sober. Was taken in tow by Steam Tug and proceeded to Sea.

July 22, 1861

Joseph Francis AB who shipped at Mauritius came on board to his duty in the place of Robert Lloyd who joined Her Majesty's Service.

Voyage from Liverpool to Rio de Janeiro

Master and Crew

Name	*Age*	*Place of Birth*	*Rank*	*Place of discharge/desertion*
Trevanion Hugo	38	Devon	Master	Liverpool
Henry Lloyd	31	Liverpool	Mate	Liverpool
William Hart	31	Scarborough	Carpenter	Liverpool
Robert Smith	34	Ayr	Boatswain	Liverpool
William Watson	24	Brecon	Steward	Liverpool
William Catley	33	Milford	Cook	Liverpool
Thomas Spencer	31	Newry	AB	Liverpool
Edward –	34	London	AB	Liverpool
James Talle	25	Jersey	AB	Liverpool
William Smyth	24	Wexford	AB	Liverpool
William McCartney	34	Belfast	AB	Liverpool
William Mathewood	26	Liverpool	AB	Liverpool
James Ames	36	Belfast	AB	Liverpool
John Collins	27	Carmarthen	AB	Liverpool
Edwin Johns	26	London	AB	Liverpool

Peter Woods	16	Cheshire	Boy	Did not board
John Finnigan	16	Liverpool	Boy	Did not board
Robert Aikin	17	Liverpool	Boy	Liverpool

Enlisted at Rio de Janeiro

William Kenyon	21	Blackburn	OS	Liverpool

Apprentices

Name	Age	Date of Indenture	Place of Indenture
William Tisdale	19	July 19, 1861	Liverpool

Official Log – Missing

Voyage from Liverpool to Bahia

Master and Crew

Name	Age	Place of Birth	Rank	Place of discharge/desertion
Archibald Johnson	49	Liverpool	Master	Liverpool (Remains)
Frederick Norris	39	Newfoundland	Mate	Liverpool
Robert Smith	36	Ayr	Boatswain	Liverpool
William Hartz	30	Scarborough	Carpenter	Liverpool
William Watson	36	Brecon	Steward	Liverpool
George Logan	41	Halifax, N.S.	Cook	Liverpool
George Smith	53	Wicklow	AB	Liverpool
Richard Worrall	28	Carlisle	AB	Bahia
John Stafford	21	Gravesend	AB	Liverpool
William Adair	25	Belfast	AB	Bahia
Charles Widdicombe	20	Exeter	AB	Liverpool
Thos. Charles –	39	Denmark	AB	Bahia
William Benson	24	Manchester	AB	Liverpool
Henry Thompson	26	Liverpool	AB	Liverpool
Thos. Henry –	22	Liverpool	AB	Liverpool

Joseph McCutcheon	15	Liverpool	OS	Liverpool
Thomas Creswell Wagstaff	17	Liverpool	Boy	Liverpool

Enlisted at Maceió

D. Shollornitz	26	Rotterdam	AB	Liverpool

Enlisted at Bahia

William Williams	36	Liverpool	AB	Bahia (Six days later)
John Wilson	22	Halifax, N.S.	OS	Liverpool
William Jones	16	Liverpool	Boy	Liverpool

Enlisted at Pernambuco

Thomas Blair	19	England	Boy	Liverpool
George Pocock	–	Bristol	Boy	Liverpool

Apprentices

Name	Date of Indenture	Place of Indenture
William Tisdale	January 19, 1860	Liverpool

Official Log – Missing

Voyage from Liverpool to Foochow

Master and Crew

Name	Age	Place of Birth	Rank	Place of discharge/desertion
Archibald Johnson	49	Liverpool	Master	London
Samuel S. Palmour	25	Pembroke	Mate	London
William Hart	32	Scarborough	Carpenter	Shanghai (Died)
Robert Smith	36	Ayr	Boatswain	London
Albert Winfield	25	St. Kitts	Steward	London
Jupiter Barrow	35	Barbados	Cook	Foochow (Jailed)
Clement le Blanc	49	Guernsey	AB	London
Thomas Galvin	22	Liverpool	AB	London
James Allen	21	Dorset	AB	London
Charles Arnaud	18	Marseilles	AB	Shanghai (Deserted)
Matthew Domingo	34	Bordeaux	AB	Shanghai (Deserted)
Michael Connolly	23	Kingston	AB	London
Peter Loyden	24	Jersey	AB	London
Joseph McCutcheon	16	Liverpool	OS	London
James Smith	21	Brighton	OS	London

Apprentices

Name	Age	Port of Indenture
Thomas Wagstaff	19	Liverpool
Henry Cosnon	16	Liverpool
Henry Dunn –	–	
John Hardwicke	18	London

Enlisted at Shanghai	Age	Part of Indenture	Rank	Place of discharge/desertion
Angus McLeod	29	Stornoway	Carpenter	London
John Galvin	18	Liverpool	OS	London
Robert Aitkins	20	Aberdeen	AB	Liverpool

Entries from the Official Log

Wednesday, August 19, 1863. Shanghae

William Hart, late Carpenter, died at Shanghae of Cholera, Wednesday, August 19, 1863.

Friday, September 4, 1863. Shanghae

About 4 p.m.

Mr. Palmour, Chief Officer, ordered the Steward to assist in loading ton Cask of Pemmican on deck for present use. He told Mr. Palmour he would not. The Mate reported him to me. I asked him if he said so. He replied he had nothing to do with getting up Pemmican and would not do it. I then ordered him out of the Cabin.

Saturday, September 12, 1863. Shanghae

Charles Arno (sic) ran away.

Matheu Domingo ran away.

October 5. Foo Chou

5 p.m

I called the Cook Aft who was walking the Deck. Asked him how he felt. He said he felt better. I then told him he had better go into the Galley in the morning to his work. He said he would.

In the morning when he was called he would not turn too (sic). The 2nd Mate brought him Aft and called me on Deck about 4 a.m. I then asked him if he meant to go to his work. He said he would not. He has done no work up to the 13th instant, but lounges about the Deck smoking his pipe.

Tuesday, October 13. Foo Chou

Jupiter Barron, Cook, left behind in jail by order of the Consul for refusing to do his Duty. Balance of his wages paid to the Consul.

April 21, 1864 to December 6, 1864

Voyage from London to Rio de Janeiro

and any other places on the East Coast of South and North America and West Indian Islands to the Continent of Europe including the Mediterranean and adjacent waters and back to the port of final discharge of cargo in the United Kingdom. Length of voyage probably twelve months.

Master and Crew

Name	Age	Place of Birth	Rank	Place of discharge/desertion
George Pepperell	25	Devon	Master	Liverpool (Remains)
Samuel Palmour	27	Pembroke	Mate	Liverpool
Robert Smith	36	Ayr	Boatswain	Liverpool
John Harvey	52	Devonport	Carpenter	Liverpool
William Corrigan	32	Dublin	Steward	Maceió
John Nelson	48	London	Cook	Maceió (Deserted)
William Griffith	20	Camaroon	AB	Rio de Janeiro
James McConnochy	29	Louth	AB	Rio de Janeiro
John B. Wall	22	St. Vincent	AB	Liverpool
William O'Brien	32	Dublin	AB	Liverpool
Alexander (?)	31	Plymouth	AB	Liverpool
Jack Smith	22	Bremen	AB	Liverpool

Will Thomas	19	Cardigan	OS	Rio de Janeiro (Deserted)
John Morris	45	Portsmouth	OS	Rio de Janeiro
John Stanley	23	Sussex	OS	Rio de Janeiro (Deserted)

Apprentices

Henry Cosnon	16
Thomas Wagstaff	19
John Hardwicke	18

Enlisted at Rio de Janeiro

José Francisco	19	Fayal	AB	Liverpool
Michel Koolsburgen	21	Rotterdam	AB	Liverpool
Matthew Donnelly	26	Liverpool	OS	Liverpool
William Cousins	23	Southampton	OS	Liverpool
John Sweet 23 Plymouth			AB	Liverpool

Enlisted at Maceió

| B. Suringa | 22 | Holland | Cook | Liverpool |

Official Log – Missing

Voyage from Liverpool to Pernambuco

and any ports and places in the Brazils and the United States, thence to a port for orders and to the Continent of Europe if required and back to a final port of discharge in the United Kingdom, the term not to exceed twelve months.

Master and Crew

Name	Age	Place of Birth	Rank	Place of discharge/desertion
George Pepperell	26	Dartmouth	Master	Liverpool (Remains)
William Williams	21	Carmarthen	Mate	Liverpool
Christian Bielsovic	33	London	Carpenter	Liverpool
Robert Smith	38	Ayr	Boatswain	Liverpool
William Hurley	20	Preston	Steward	Liverpool
James Fish	21	Blackpool	Cook	Liverpool
Peter Wilson	27	Trieste	AB	Liverpool
Nicholas George	23	Trieste	AB	Liverpool
Charles Seldon	31	Bristol	AB	Liverpool
Richard Guinness	21	Ramsey	AB	Liverpool
Thomas Stall	24	Liverpool	AB	Liverpool
August Coombs	27	Nova Scotia	AB	Liverpool

| John Cousins | 19 | Halifax | OS | Liverpool |
| John Lynch | 21 | Liverpool | OS | Liverpool |

Apprentices

Name	Age	Place of Indenture
John Walker Hardwicke	15	London
Thomas Creswel Wagstaff	17	Liverpool
Henry Casnon	15	Liverpool

Official Log – Missing

May 28, 1865 to November 25, 1865.

Voyage from Liverpool to Nuevo Bay, Patagonia

and any ports and places in the Atlantic, Pacific and Indian Oceans, thence to a port for orders and to the Continent if required, and back to a final port of discharge in the United Kingdom, term not to exceed two years.

Master and Crew

Name	Age	Place of Birth	Rank	Place of discharge/desertion
George Pepperell	25	Dartmouth	Master	Liverpool (Remains)
John Downes	39	Isle of Man	Mate	Liverpool
Matthew Burgess	24	Macclesfield	Boatswain	Liverpool
James Fish	22	Blackpool	Steward	Liverpool
John Smith	39	Wilmington	Head Cook	Liverpool
Alexander Nolan	33	Troon	AB	Liverpool
Owen Williams	24	Anglesey	AB	Liverpool
Joseph Leonard	27	Guernsey	AB	Liverpool
Francis Mitchell	20	Arbroath	AB	New Bay (Deserted)
Owen Riley	32	Waterford	AB	Did not board
Lars Petterson	25	Sweden	OS	Liverpool
Matthew Warren	20	St. John, N.B.	OS	Liverpool

Thomas William Nassau Greene	21	Kildare, Ireland	Surgeon	New Bay
Thomas Evans	29	Montgomery	Passenger Steward	Did not board
Amos Williams	25	Carnarvon	Passenger Cook	New Bay
Richard Jones Berwyn	27	Merioneth	Purser	New Bay
Robert Nagle	32	Barmouth	Passenger Steward	New Bay
Antonio Silva	59	Cape Verde	AB	Liverpool

Apprentices

Name	Age	Place of Indenture	Date of Indenture
John Walker Hardwicke	15	London	9 November, 1861
Henry Cosnon	15	Liverpool	20 March, 1863
Thomas Creswell	17	Liverpool	5 June, 1862

Births, Marriages and Deaths (taken from the Official Log)
Births

Date of Birth	Name of Child	Name of Father	Name of Mother	Profession or Occupation of Father
June 11	Morgan Jones	John Jones	Mary Morgan	Collier
June 25	Rachel Jenkins	Aaron Jenkins	Rachel Evans	Collier

Marriages

Date Married	Names of both Parties	Ages	Status	Occupation	Father's Name & Occupation
June 2	William Hughes	33	Widower	Stonemason	Robert Hughes – Stonemason
June 2	Ann Lewis	35	Widow	Servant	Robert Pugh – Cabinet Maker

Deaths other than those of Crew

Date of Death	Name of Deceased	Age	Parents' Names	Cause of Death
June 9	Catherine Jane Thomas	2	Robt. & Mary Thomas	Croup
June 10	James Jenkins	2	Aaron & Rachel Jenkins	Cancrum Oris of the Mouth
June 28	John Davis	11 mths.	Robt. & Catherine Davis	Water on the Brain
July 17	Elizabeth Solomon	13 mths.	Griffith & Eliz. Solomon	Acute Bronchitis

Entries from the Official Log

Saturday, May 27, 1865. Liverpool

Owen O'Reilly AB (American) who signed agreement to proceed (on) the Voyage has not made his appearance. consequently have shipped Antonio Silva AB in his stead.

Friday, June 2, 1865

Noon.

William Hughes of Angelsey, Stone Mason, and Ann Lewis, Widower, were today united in the Bonds of Holy Matrimony by Rev. L. Humphries in the presence of Thomas Ellis and John Morgan, Witnesses.

Friday, June 9, 1865

7.30 p.m.

At 7.30 p.m. Catherine Jane, infant, daughter of Robert and Mary Thomas, died of Croup, aged 2 years.

Saturday, June 10, 1865

10 a.m.

Committed the body of the above infant to the Deep. Funeral Rites performed by the Chaplain of the Colony.

Saturday, June 10, 1865

10 p.m.

At 10 p.m. James, youngest son of Aron and Rachel Jenkins, died of Cancrum Oris of the Mouth, aged 2½ years.

Sunday, 11 June, 1865.

8 a.m.

Committed the body of the above child to the Deep with Funeral Rites.

Wednesday, June 28, 1865

2 a.m.

At 2 a.m. John, infant son of Robert and Catherine Davis, died of Chronic Hydrocephalus, Water on the Brain, aged 11 months.

At 8 a.m. Committed the body of the infant to the Deep. Funeral Rites performed by the Chaplain of the Colony.

Monday, 17 July, 1865

8 p.m.

At 8 p.m. Elizabeth, infant daughter of Griffiths and Elizabeth Solomon, died of Acute Bronchitis.

Tuesday, 18 July, 1865

8 a.m.

Committed the body of the above infant to the Deep. Funeral Rites performed by the Revd. L. Humphries, Minister of the Colony.

Monday, July 31, 1865. Nueva Bay, Patagonia

This day by mutual agreement the under–mentioned persons have been discharged from the barque "Mimosa", having landed all the passengers.

Thos. Greene, M.D.

Robt. Neagle, Passengers Steward

Richard Berwyn, Purser

Amos Williams, Passengers Cook.

All these persons remaining in the Colony.

Thursday, September 7, 1865. Nueva Bay, Patagonia

This evening one of the boat's Crew, Francis Mitchell AB absconded from the Boat, and taking all his effects with him, and has since become a Deserter.

December 13, 1865 to May 5, 1866.

Voyage from Liverpool to Bahia

and any port and places in South and North America (thence to a port for order and to the Continent if required) and back to a final port of discharge in the United Kingdom, term not to exceed 12 months.

Master and Crew

Name	Age	Place of Birth	Rank	Place of discharge/desertion
George Pepperell	27	Dartmouth	Master	Liverpool (Remains)
John Downes	39	Isle of Man	Mate	Liverpool
William Hopkins	24	Durham	Boatswain	Liverpool
Robert Coulson	53	Durham	Carpenter	Liverpool
James Fish	22	Blackpool	Steward	Liverpool
Peter Gore	26	Glasgow	Cook	Liverpool
Robert Henry	32	Donegal	AB	Liverpool
James Sheenan	36	Wicklow	AB	Liverpool
Henry Bellow	31	Liverpool	AB	Liverpool
Colin Campbell	24	Shaftesbury	AB	Liverpool
Charles Davies	22	Cork	AB	Liverpool
Carl Schmidt	31	Austria	AB	Liverpool
Edward Strange	22	Gloucester	OS	Liverpool

| Matthew Warren | 19 | St. John | OS | Liverpool |
| John Williams | 19 | St. Kitts | OS | Drowned |

Apprentices

| Henry Cosnon | 15 | | | Maceió (Deserted) |
| Thomas Wagstaff | 17 | | | |

Enlisted at Maceió

| Robert Carruthers | 22 | – | AB | Liverpool |

Entries from the Official Log

Wednesday, October 15, 1865. Prince's Pier Head.

6 a.m.

Hanked the Ship to Pier Head. Crew came on board, one of which, James Sheenan AB, was very much Intoxicated and unfit for work and remained so untill (sic) the following day, thereby not fulfilling the agreement, viz.: to join the Ship sober. On the morning of the following day he went to his duty.

Monday, October 25, 1865

4.00. p.m

On calling the watch at 4 p.m. the order was given to Tack Ship. James Sheenan did not come aft untill (sic) called and when remonstrated with by Mr. Wm. Hopkins, 2nd Mate, he became very abusive, also to myself and 2nd Mate, when to avoid any disturbance in the Ship I was compelled to send (the) man, Sheenan, from the Poop (deck).

Tuesday, October 19, 1865

Today have found that James Sheenan AB is in some points unable to perform his duty owing to bad sight. He cannot see, even to steer the Ship, without the aid of glasses and then very imperfectly, totally unfitting him to perform the most essential part of his duty, viz. (to) keep a good lookout. This is a very great want on the part of a Seaman shipped as an efficient and Able Bodied man. Even when steering he cannot see the compass.

Tuesday, October 19, 1865

Today complaints have been made against Peter Gore,Cook, as on former occasions. Today he has completely spoiled the Ship's Company's dinner, the Flour made into pudding being totally unfit for food. On former occasions he has proved himself incompetent to perform the Duties of Cook, and although still remaining attending to the Galley (he not being fit for any other duty) the crew have to prepare all their own food, the Steward doing the cooking for the Cabin.

Monday, January 1, 1866

John Williams OS sent aloft on the Main Yard to assist in rigging out (the) Topmast Studding Boom. He by some means missed his hold and fell from the Yard, striking the Fore Brace Bump Pin and Block. In falling he fell overboard. A Life Buoy was thrown to him. Ship rounded too (sic) and Boat lowered, and in less than 4 minutes had left the Ship with the 2 Officers and 3 Crew. They immediately pulled to the Spot, but of no avail.Nothing could be seen of him. After being away from the Ship 45 minutes (they) returned to the Ship. She was accordingly kept on her course again. We are of (the) opinion (that) he was killed by striking the Block and Bump Pin.

Immediately on the return of the Boat to the Ship sent Mr. Hopkins, 2nd Officer, to see (to) all the effects of the deceased Seaman, John Williams, the following being a correct list of them.

1 Pea Jacket, 1 Coat, 2 prs. Trousers, 1 Cotton Shirt, 2 Woollen Shirts, 1 Guernsey Shirt, 1 Blue Flannel Shirt, 2 Mufflers, 2 Flannel Singlets, 2 prs. Drawers, 1 Towel, 1 Straw Hat, 1 Sou Wester (sic), 2 prs. Woollen Stockings, 1 Prayer Book, 1 Needle Case & Needles, 1 Blanket, 1 pr. Boots, 1 Bag containing the same.

Tuesday, March 20, 1866. Pernambuco
Sent the Apprentice Henry Cosnon in the Boat for Chief Officer (to come aboard from Pernambuco). While waiting a few minutes, (he) ran away from the Boat. On coming on board I was informed of it. Had an examination of his berth and chest, both of which was empty, he not returning to the Ship. I have every reason to believe he deserted.

Thursday, March 22, 1866. Pernambuco
Shipped Robert Carruthers AB after the Ship was cleared, who joined according to Agreement.

May 5, 1866. Liverpool
Came to an anchor in the river Mersey, this ending the Voyage.

Voyage from Liverpool to Bahia

and any ports and places in the Brazils, thence to a port for orders and to the Continent if required and back to a final port of discharge in the United Kingdom. Term not to exceed 12 months.

Master and Crew

Name	Age	Place of Birth	Rank	Place of discharge/desertion
George Pepperell	27	Dartmouth	Master	Liverpool (Remains)
Richard Ewald	30	Prussia	Mate	Liverpool
George Mudford	28	London	Boatswain	Discharged before sailing
James Clark `	28	London	Boatswain	Liverpool
John School	29	?	Carpenter	Liverpool
John Henry	26	St. Helens	Steward	Pernambuco
Richard Edwards	32	Falmouth	Cook	Liverpool
Samuel Smith	30	Canterbury	AB	Liverpool
Jacob Smith	23	Hanover	AB	Liverpool
William Evans	27	Falmouth	AB	Liverpool
Lewis Thomas	32	Leith	AB	Liverpool
Henry Bellow	31	Liverpool	AB	Liverpool
Antonio Silva	40	Cape Verde	OS	Liverpool

Joseph Smith	22	Liverpool	OS	Bahia
Matthew Warren	20	St. John, N.B.	OS	Drowned
Richard Walley	15	Manchester	Boy	Liverpool
Hugh Cox	15	Ireland	Boy	Liverpool

Enlisted at Pernambuco

| Michael McClintock | 16 | Glasgow | | |

Entries from the Official Log

Friday, June 15, 1866. Liverpool. On Board in Dock.

11a.m

The Vessel not having completed her cargo in consequence of bad weather the Ship's Company declined working.

Saturday, June 16, 1866. Liverpool

11 a.m.

None of the Ship's Company joined the Ship today giving same (reason).

Sunday, June 17, 1866. Liverpool.

11 a.m.

None of the Ship's Company on board today.

Monday, June 18, 1866. Liverpool

Today the following persons have joined the Ship as per Agreement. Viz: Richard Ewald, Chief Officer, John Henry, Steward, John School, Carpenter, Henry Bellow AB, Antonio Silva AB, Richard Walley, Boy, and Hugh Cox, Boy.

This day at 3 p.m. discharged George Mudford, Boatswain, by mutual agreement and shipped James Clark, 2nd Mate (Substitute).

Tuesday, June 19, 1866. Liverpool

11 a.m.

No persons being on board but Mr. R. Ewald, 1st Mate, John Henry, Steward, John School, Carpenter, Richard Edwards, Cook, Joseph Smith OS, and the two Boys, employed riggers to haul the ship to Pier Head. After the Ship being there and fast to the steam tug the remainder of the Ship's Company jumped on board.

4.30 p.m.

Mustered the Crew and found them all correct. Came to an anchor in the Mersey.

Wednesday, June 20, 1866. River Mersey

2.30 a.m.

The steam tug "Wonder" came alongside. Got underweigh and proceeded on our Voyage. Pilot and tug left the Ship at the Bell Buoy at 6.15 a.m., the former taking back the Crew Return List. All on board.

Sunday, July 1, 1866. At Sea

James Clark, 2nd Mate, complains of being sick, violent shiverings, heat, severe pains in the back and head and vomitting. Not able to do duty in consequence. On inquiring if he had any known complaint or any disorder he knows of, he told me no and assured me he did not know what was wrong with himself, and as those symptoms correspond with the Smallpox I treated him according to the Medical Guide for that complaint. Remained off duty.

Monday, July 2, 1866

After 8 a.m. James Clark again came on deck, but (was) obliged to go below by 11 a.m.after suffering (he says) from violent pains in the back, and all the symptoms of yesterday on again. Asking him if he had any other complaint he assured me he had not but was suffering from a blow received on one of his legs which struck him when coming out of dock in letting go the Stern rope. This he told when I told him he was walking as if something was amiss with him. Off duty.

Tuesday, July 3, 1866
Still off duty.

Wednesday, July 4, 1866

This morning James Clark came on deck to his duty, but before his watch was up (was) sent below again and remained off duty.

Thursday, July 5, 1866

J. Clark complaining of suffering great agony during the night past and whilst in the cabin for his medicine acknowledged that he was suffering from a Stricture. The only excuse he made for not having dealt candidly with me in the first instance of his being sick (was that) he did not like to idle. Off duty and remains to watch.

Saturday, July 21, 1866

8 p.m.

James Clark again took charge of his watch.

Tuesday, July 24

At 11.45 p.m. I came on deck and found J. Clark, officer of the watch, asleep upon the (deck) house. To excuse himself from this he informed me (that) he was not able to keep on his legs. Sent him off duty where he remained untill (sic) the arrival of the Ship at Bahia.

Thursday, July 26. Bahia.

On the morning after my arrival I sent for James Clark and told him (that) if he was not able to go to his duty he had better go to the hospital which he coincided with as he informed me (that) he was not able to do his duty. Accordingly he went to the hospital and remained there until Saturday, August 1st, when he again came on board the ship and went to his duty. On my arrival at Bahia all the foregoing entries were distinctly read to him as I told him I intended to stop his wages while off duty according to the Act.

Sunday, August 26, 1866. Bahia

This morning at 10 a.m. I left the Ship in the Gig with 4 hands. 2 of my crew knowing I was going to Church asked leave to go (too) which was granted them. Left 2 others to look after the boat. On my return from church, seeing an Ordinary Seaman, Joseph Smith, very much Intoxicated, I said nothing to him, not wishing to notice it, it being the Sabbath. On coming alongside of the Ship, I told him to remain in the boat as I had no wish for him, being intoxicated, to be with the remainder of the Crew, they being sober. He insisted on coming on board after both lst and 2nd Officers telling him to remain where he was, or else I should be forced to put him in the fore Cabin until sober. (When) he was called Aft he became Very impertinent and abusive, and, when on the poop, he assaulted and struck me, tearing my coat, and knocked my hat off. This was more than I could quietly stand. I closed with him and threw him and had a pair of Irons put on his wrists and put (him) into the fore Cabin. About 10 minutes, after having no wish whatever of punishing him any further than keeping him away from the rest of the Crew, he was asleep or fained (sic) to be. I sent the Steward into the Fore Cabin to take the Irons off him, he then being quiet. The Irons he had slipped off his wrists, and so I let him remain, telling him (that) he must stay in the Fore Cabin. About 3 o'clock he made his escape into the Forecastle. When the officers again went to bring him aft he became very abusive and called them very bad names and used such language not fit to be written. He struck the 2nd Officer, James Clark, when he got two or three blows from him and was with great difficulty again brought aft. He became very uproarious, making a great noise and using all kinds of threats to Captain and Officers and also saying (that) amongst other places he had been in one was a lunatic asylum and when there they could not confine him, swearing he would cut our Bloody Livers out, and in fact his conduct all throughout appeared more like a lunatic than a sane person. After he was placed below in the Fore Cabin he made another blow at my head. I lifted my arm to defend it and received a sharp blow on the back part of my right hand with something he had in his hand. What it was I cannot tell, nor can the Carpenter, the only person present. But as soon as I was struck I knocked him down, when he was again put in Irons (and) the Fore Cabin secured and locked. He still continued using threats and most vile language until about 7 p.m. About 8.30

p.m. the Mate complained to me that he was trying to pick the lock on the door and that he considered it not safe for any person to be asleep in the Cabin without first making Smith secure. I called the 2nd Officer and (the) Carpenter. They, along with myself, thought Smith not responsible for his actions. If he ever entered the Cabin whilst we were asleep he could easily posses (sic) himself of a cutlass from the stand. He was accordingly secured for the night so that he could do no harm or hurt himself.

All through those proceedings above stated I particularly requested the Officers to use no violence whatever, but merely to secure him.

Monday, August 27, 1866

At 5.30 a.m. I ordered James Clark, the 2nd Officer, to release Smith and told him to go to his duty, which he refused on plea of not being able.

(At) 8 a.m., he having overheard my intentions of bringing him before the Consulate, he told me (that) he was very sorry for what occurred and agreed to beg pardon of the 1st and 2nd Officer, to pay for my coat and medical advice for my hand which is altogether helpless. He returned to his duty, but at 2 p.m. he knocked off and remained below until the 30th, when he made a request to be allowed to see the Consul, which was accordingly granted him. Since we have been in Bahia he has frequently disobeyed my orders. When told to go to the Ship after heeding me he has proceeded a short distance and then returned again to the shore and has gone on shore without leave.

The above entries have been made by the Mate as the Captain cannot write through the injury to his hand inflicted by J. Smith. The above entries here duly been read over to him in presence of witnesses.

Thursday, August 30, 1866. Bahia

At the British Consulate this day discharged Joseph Smith OS, he complaining of being sick and not fit to proceed in this Ship. Discharged on those grounds.

Tuesday, October 30. Pernambuco

This day discharged John Henry, Steward, having again caught him in the act of stealing. Turned him out of the Cabin last night, drunk and abusive. The following day the Chief and 2nd Officer and Carpenter with myself appeared at the British Consulate and proved he had taken a great many articles away with him yesterday when he took his effects on shore from the Ship, amongst which were sundry articles of my own clothing.

The above mentioned discharged at the British Consulate and imprisoned for Robbery.

Thursday, November 22, 1866. Pernambuco

Today at the office of the British Consulate shipped Michael McClintock, Boy, who at once proceeded on board.

Monday, October 15, 1866

This day Matthew Warren, OS, went on shore to the Hospital with Secondary Symptoms Venereal.

Thursday, November 22, 1866

This day the above mentioned Matthew Warren OS came on board the ship and returned to his duty.

Monday, December 17, 1866

On Monday the 17th inst. at 4. a.m. ship running before a gale from SSW and a heavy sea running and very dark, Matthew Warren was missed from the deck. Some time had elapsed before it was found that he had fallen overboard. The Boy, Michael McClintock, says, "I was at work with him and he got on the Ship rail to let go a rope", and he never saw the deceased afterwards. There was no one aloft at the time but the watch at necessary work about the decks. I, the Master, had been on deck all night and running between the Islands of Terceira and St. Miguel, the Azores. I heard someone shout. Thinking it to be the Officer of the watch who was on the Forecastle, I hailed to know what was the matter. This shout must have been the drowning man as he passed astern of the Ship. The man at the wheel did not hear it, and after a while the aforesaid Boy, recovering from his fright on finding the man not there, gave the alarm of a man overboard. But alas! No one saw him fall nor could they see him in the Water. There was not the slightest possibility of saving the poor fellow's life for the night was very dark, not a star visible, the sky overcast and the Ship running at the rate of 12 knots per hour and a heavy sea running, and he must have been some distance astern even when the alarm was given for some time had elapsed before our voice could have been understood amidst the noise of the storm.

During the day Matthew Warren's (deceased) effects were all collected together and put into his chest, locked and removed to the Fore Cabin.

Voyage from Liverpool to Pernambuco

any any ports and places in the Brazils and back to a final port of discharge in the United Kingdom. Term not to exceed 12 months.

Master and Crew

Name	Age	Place of Birth	Rank	Place of discharge/desertion
George Pepperell	28	Dartmouth	Master	Liverpool (Remains)
Richard Ewald	31	Prussia	Mate	Liverpool
John Walker Hardwicke	21	London	Boatswain	Liverpool
James Cowan	30	London	Carpenter	Liverpool
Richard Edwards	31	Falmouth	Steward	Liverpool
John Henry	36	Derby	Cook	Liverpool
Daniel MacCarthy	33	Ireland	AB	Did not board
Robert Williams	38	Grenock	AB	Liverpool
Henry Patterson	33	Norway	AB	Liverpool
T. Dekker	25	Amsterdam	AB	Liverpool
J. Guttinger	32	Holland	AB	Liverpool
Edward Harrison	17	Longford	OS	Liverpool
Louis Williams	21	Jamaica	OS	Liverpool

Henry Barnett	20	Jamaica	OS	Liverpool
William Davidson	14	London	Boy	Liverpool
Pedro Patterson	37	Sweden	AB	Liverpool

Entries from the Official Log

February 23, 1867. Liverpool

Signed Articles of Agreement.

Thursday, February 26, 1867. Liverpool

The Crew joined the Ship, all joining except Daniel McCarthy AB. Shipped Pedro Patterson in his Room.

April 7, 1867

Arrived at Pernambuco.

Friday, May 10, 1867. Pernambuco

Since the Ship has been in this port R. Edwards, Steward, has knocked off work several times, generally in the latter part of the day, and complained of being lightheaded and giddy. The Officers (lst and 2nd Mate) are of opinion (that) the cause is Drink, for he lies down and is with great difficulty aroused to take medicine. After(wards) he seems to sleep as soundly as any person in the Ship, yet he cannot work. Complains of Billiousness on these occasions. The Officers (lst & 2nd Mate) have informed me that in their opinion he was under the influence of intoxicating Drink and not sick. I must also state (that) this man has repeatedly neglected his duty and allowed his pantry to become in a filthy and disgusting state, inasmuch that one of the OS has had to be sent down from deck to clean it. In some of the shelfs (sic) Live Maggots (were) crawling about. This was shown to me by Mr. Ewald, Chief Mate. Since this discovery have had a more vigilant lookout kept on his movements which he appears to dislike and to resent.

On the same day I observed him doing nothing on deck and asked him if his pantry was clean, when he was very impertinent and insolent and told me he would knock off and I could go to the Consul as soon as possible and get his discharge the following morning.

Saturday, May 11, 1867
Knocked off duty and asked for leave to see the Consul which was granted. The Consul told him to go on board and go to his work. I also saw the Consul and it being mail day he told me to bring the man on shore on Monday if he would not work Saturday.

For refusal of duty after coming on board, two day's pay.

Sunday, 12 May, 1867. Pernambuco
R. Edwards still refused to go to his duty for which stop pay according to the Act.

Monday, May 13, 1867. Pernambuco
R. Edwards returned to his duty as Steward with promises of amendment. In consequence of his doing so do not take him to the Consul.

Saturday, May 18, 1867. Pernambuco

At 8 a.m. as usual went to breakfast and at 9.30 a.m., observing the breakfast things still on the table called the Steward R. Edwards to clear away. For some time he could not be found, but discovered laying asleep on some sails in the Fore Cabin, intoxicated. After difficulty he was aroused and he told me he was Drunk. On the 1st Mate, Mr. Ewald, remonstrating with him, he said, "Well, I told the Captain I was drunk, and what more does he want?" Gave him an emetic and he remained incapable this day.

Drunk and incapable, two days pay.

On his getting sober he complained of Billiousness, but evidently by the effects of his late intoxication and remained off duty.

Sunday, May 19th, 1867. Left Pernambuco
(R. Edwards) off duty through drink.

R. Edwards has again committed himself by being drunk and neglecting his duty. On my finding him again in this state he acknowledged it and told me he gets the drink from shore, but would not tell me who brought it to him. This is his own avowal, but it seems strange as I have not given him any money since being in this port.

Wednesday, May 22, 1867. Between Pernambuco and Maceió
Called the Steward, R. Edwards to see what Preserved Meats was (sic) in the cabin and found 4 2-lb tins short. The Tins were all right in Pernambuco, and as he cannot give any account of the missing meats I think this might be the means of his getting the Drink to get intoxicated so often in Pernambuco. The above Meats are missing.

Friday, May 24, 1867. Maceió

After dinner R. Edwards again refused duty. I was on shore at the time, but he told the 1st. Mate he would do no more work in the Cabin whilst in the Ship. It was too hot. He could not stand it. On my coming on board I sent for him and in the presence of the 1st. Mate, Mr. Ewald, he told me he would not do any more work in the Cabin and I may disrate him or do anything I chose to him, but no more work for him in the Cabin, which leaves me no other alternative than to disrate him, he knowing at the same time (that) I could not, if I wished, get another Steward in his place, this being only a small port. But as he has hitherto proved himself (by the foregoing charges) incapable of the duty of Steward (because) of incompetency and Drunkenness I shall from this day disrate him to be an AB or OS as his qualifications (together with my Officers) may decide.

May 27, 1867. Maceió

Although having my full complement of ABs on board and having put a Boy (J. Maxwell) in the place of the late Steward, R. Edwards, who has been disrated as above, think that if he is able to perform an AB's duty will give him that rating. The 1st Mate, Mr. Ewald gave him a rope to splice, "Long Splice", which he could not do after being ¾ of an hour over it. 1st and 2nd Mate both witnessed his inability to make a splice. Neither could he flemish coil a rope.

Saturday, August 18, 1867. Off Holyhead

Now at the conclusion of the Voyage I feel bound to acknowledge that he has not proved himself competent to do an AB duty, but is only entitled to an OS pay dateing (sic) from the day on which he refused to do any more duty in the Cabin. At the same time I feel bound to state that the Boy, J. Maxwell, has done Steward duty since the above R. Edwards was disrated, but owing to his subsequent good conduct as OS will not enforce the fines.

Voyage from Liverpool to Bahia

and any Ports or Places in South or North America and the West Indies, thence to a port for orders and to the Continent if required and back to a final port of discharge in the United Kingdom. Term not to exceed 12 months.

Master and Crew

Name	Age	Place of Birth	Rank	Place of discharge/desertion
George Pepperell	28	Dartmouth	Master	Liverpool (Remains)
Henry King Forrest	32	Cork	Mate	Did not board
John Walker Hardwicke	21	London	Boatswain	Liverpool
Thomas Doran	25	Co. Down	Carpenter	Liverpool
James White	22	Birmingham	Steward	Liverpool
Henry Perman	25	Warminster	Cook	Liverpool
John Sulvey	23	Trieste	AB	Did not board
William Rogers	25	Liverpool	AB	Bahia (Deserted)
Joseph Pomeroy	21	Falmouth	AB	Did not board
John Smith	28	Halifax	AB	Liverpool
James Burchell	26	Crosshaven	AB	Liverpool
Thomas Hayland	21	Glasgow	AB	Pernambuco
Thomas Stonson	18	Liverpool	OS	Liverpool

David Bedford	17	London	Boy	Liverpool
George Williams	21	Ohio	AB	Pernambuco
William Berry	33	Pembroke	Mate	Liverpool
John Muncaster	29	Lancashire	AB	Liverpool
C. Carlson	25	Hamburg	AB	Liverpool
Charles Anderson	25	New York	AB	Liverpool
Richard Rawley	?	America	AB	Pernambuco

Supernumerary

| George Charly | | Stowaway | | Sailor |

Entries from the Official Log

Monday, October 21, 1867. Liverpool

3.45 a.m.

The Ship having been hauled to the Pier Head and Steam Tug fast, Pilot on board. Discovered we were short our complement of hands, the following being the members of the crew who did not join the ship. Viz: Henry King Forrest, Mate, Joseph Pomeroy AB, John Sulvey AB.

Kept the ship in the river while substitutes were obtained in the places. Shipped the following:

William Berry, First Mate, Richard Rawley AB, George Williams AB.

After shipping those new, the Ship proceeded on her voyage, the two last-named Seamen each receiving an advance of £2 10 0 (by advance note).

Monday, October 28, 1867

4 p.m.

Called the Mate, Mr.Berry, and the substitutes, Richard Rawley and Geo. Williams aft and after reading the Articles of Agreement over to them the Mate, Mr. Berry and Geo. Williams signed, but Richard Rawley refused to sign them.

Monday October 28, 1867

8 a.m.

Although the Crew has had the Articles of Agreement distinctly read over to them with the Board of Trade Regulations adopted and have all been told individually by myself and Officers, still James Burchell AB will persist in wearing a Sheath Knife which I have again cautioned him against wearing and against the rules adopted. He having disobeyed these orders on several occasions, I shall now from this date enforce the Fine, viz.

James Burchell, AB, for wearing Sheath Knife, one day's pay £0 – 1 – 8.

Wednesday, November 6, 1867

2 p.m.

Having occasion to speak to Richard Rawley on account of laziness which he has shown on several occasions he became very insolent and with sundry speeches told me he did not care a damn for me and did not come here to be humbugged, neither did he want any of my lip.

One day's pay for contemptuous language, £0 − 1 − 8.

Thursday, November 7, 1867

12.30 noon.

Again I have to order James Burchell to discontinue wearing a Sheath Knife, he having one on.

James Burchell for wearing Sheath Knife, one day's pay £0 − 1 − 8.

Sunday, November 10, 1867

9 a.m.

The Crew having all agreed to adopt the Board of Trade regulations and have been ordered not to wash clothes on the Sabbath (no work being done on board that day), Richard Rawley persists in washing clothes against orders, considering that he is free as he refuses to sign the Articles, although I have told him I have the same claim on him as the other members of the Crew, showing a total disregard for this and several other orders given to him.

Richard Rawley for washing clothes on a Sunday, one day's pay £0 – 1 – 8.

For disobeying lawful commands two days pay £0 – 3 – 4.

Sunday, November 24, 1867

9 a.m.

Again Richard Rawley persists in washing clothes contrary to the regulations adopted.

Washing clothes, one day's pay £0 – 1 – 8.

Monday, November 25, 1867

3.45 a.m. to 4 a.m.

This morning about 4 o'clock I was awoke by a noise upon (the) deck just over my head, and upon going on deck to ascertain the cause, the lst Mate, Mr. Wm. Berry stated that having made sail he called the watch aft which consists of 2 ABs, W. Rogers AB and 2 Boys. After waiting some time and finding only a Boy come aft, he went to see for the others. When he called Rogers and spoke to him about his not attending to the Mate's call he (Rogers) became very Insolent and Abusive and also used threatening language and trying to provoke a quarrel. As I came up the Cabin stairs I distinctly heard him call (to) the Mate "A Son of a Bitch, I'll double you up." This was heard also by both 2nd Mate, Mr Hardwicke and the Carpenter who were also awakened with the noise on the Poop, the man Rogers acting the Bully to the fullest sense of the term, and attacked the Mate most furiously. When I ordered him to go to his duty he also refused to (obey) me as he had previously done to the Mate and using abusive language, said he would do no more in the Ship for he had done the last stroke of work on board. I told him if he would not to to his work I would punish him and keep him in confinement. He still refused duty. I then went below for a pair of Handcuffs and while I was gone he went off the Poop and somewhere forward, apparently to arm himself with something, and immediately returned again. He made a rush at the Mate, swearing he would do for him, and struck him (the Mate) a sharp blow on the left eye brow and felled him. The Mate called out, "He has cut me with something," for the mark which was about 2 inches long in this form, Y, so that it were impossible to inflict this with the hand, and as soon as he had done it he must have thrown it overboard as it was dark at the time. An inch lower would have caused the Mate the loss of his eye. Force had to be used, but not with violence.

I had him immediately handcuffed and brought below to the Cabin. The only available place he could be put for security was the Lazaretto untill (sic) daylight when he was released and left in the Cabin untill a place could be made convenient in the Fore Cabin which caused some delay as it was now filled with cargo, but as soon as it was made ready had him place below in the Fore Cabin, directly under the hatchway so that he may have plenty of ventilation.

After due and careful investigation of this case with my officers, lst & 2nd Mate and Carpenter, we consider that from the vindictiveness of Roger's behaviour towards the Mate in trying to do him bodily injury and his threatening language, we are of opinion that it would be dangerous to let him go at large and therefore feel justified in keeping him a prisoner untill able to hand him over to the law as a desperate character. May attack an officer in the nightime and do him an injury or take his life unawares.

His general conduct is not good, always dissatisfied and a man who apparently could lead all the others in the Forecastle and who I believe to have already stirred up discontent amongst them and therefore feel it my duty to punish this man and to make an example of him as far as the Merchant Shipping Act will admit. Section 243. Art. 4.6.5.

The above charges have been distinctly read over to Wm. Rogers in our presence and we hereby affix our signatures.

Sunday, December 1, 1867

9 a.m.

Again Richard Rawley persists in washing clothes contrary to the regulations.

Washing clothes on Sunday, one day's pay £0 − 1 − 8.

Monday, December 2nd, 1867

8 a.m.

Again James Burchell will persist in wearing the Sheath Knife and have every reason (to think that) he does this because he has been cautioned not to do so.

James Burchell for wearing a sheath knife, one day's pay £0 − 1 − 8.

Continued disobedience to lawful commands, two day's pay £0 − 3 − 4.

Saturday, December 7, 1867

11 a.m.

Arrived at this port and it is mutually agreed between Wm. Rogers and the Master (that) as soon as the said Wm. Rogers has worked out the pay due to the Master for sundries supplied, viz: tobacco, clothing, etc. £2 − 7 − 3, and the Mate Mr. Berry not wanting to prosecute him, he shall be discharged from the Ship

December 10, 1867. Bahia

Again Richard Rawley has been requested to sign the Ship's Articles, but still refuses.

Saturday, December 21, 1867. Bahia

Noon.

Again James Burchell is wearing a Sheath Knife, although the Crew have been employed in discharging cargo, consequently no occasion for wearing such an article. On being told by the 2nd Mate, Mr. Hardwicke to take it off, he made use of impertinent and contemptuous language and asked him who the devil he was to order him. The Mate hearing this interfered, and he also gave him (the Mate) a great deal of Insolence.

Saturday evening. Bahia

8 p.m.

James Burchell came aft and asked for his discharge which was refused. Rather an unreasonable hour, 8 p.m. Saturday night, and we are of belief (that) he came with the intention of provoking a quarrel as he could have no reasonable excuse for demanding this at such an hour. Ordered him to go forward which he did very reluctantly.

Tuesday, December 24, 1867. Bahia

This day allowed Wm. Rogers to go on Shore to the British Consulate having now worked out the above named sum being due to the Master for goods supplied.

Friday, January 3, 1868. Bahia

6 p.m.

Not having seen anything of Wm. Rogers since the day on which he landed or of his having applied for his discharge, I have come to the conclusion that he has deserted taking his effects with him.

Friday, January 3, 1868

6 p.m.

Sailed from Bahia for Pernambuco Roads.

Monday, January 6, 1868

11 a.m.

John Smith AB whilst in the act of whitewashing the t'ween decks fell off onto the Lower Hold hurting both feet so much that he was unable to walk off duty. Treated him according to instructions in Medical Guide for sprained ankle.

Wednesday, January 15, 1868, Pernambuco Roads.

8 a.m.

Having arrived yesterday in the Roads and laying at a single anchor, the wind blowing dead on the Shore, ordered an anchor watch to be kept, consisting of one man of one hour each. At 12 o'clock midnight Thomas Stonson OS called Thos. Hayland AB whose watch was from 12 to 1 o'clock who relieved him and told him it was all right. He afterwards deliberately went to his hammock and went to sleep. This I consider to be a piece of gross negligence as it must be with (the) intention of going to sleep that he went to his hammock.

For being asleep on the look out, two days pay £0 – 3 – 4.

For wilful disobedience to lawful commands, two days pay £0 – 3 – 4.

And we are of opinion that an act of this kind (he being in charge of the ship whilst on watch and only about a mile off the reef) ought to severely punished.

The above fines have been rescinded, not having any wages due him.

Thursday, January 16, 1868. Pernambuco
10 a.m.
Requested the attendance of the Medical Officer of the British Hospital at this port to look at and examine the hurt received by John Smith, AB, as he still continues unable to walk. Consequently off duty.

Thursday, January 16, 1868. Pernambuco
Having again occasion to speak to Richard Rawley on account of laziness, he not working as he ought, he wanted to know if I wanted him to work like a nigger and became very Insolent and Abusive, telling me he wanted to go on shore and see the Consul tomorrow, alleging that I was under a penalty for keeping him, that he had been shanghaid on board this ship contrary to his consent.

For insolence and contemptuous language, one day's pay £0 – 1 – 8.

The above fine is rescinded together with the others against him, he not having any wages due him.

Friday, January 17, 1868. Pernambuco
6 a.m.

On the Crew being called to their work this morning (discharging Ballast) the following members refused duty alleging (that) they wanted to see the British Consul and would not work untill they had done so.

James Burchell AB, Thomas Hayland AB, Richard Rawley AB and George Williams AB.

They then went on shore and I employed labourers in their room.

At the Consulate it was agreed that they should each be discharged (with the exception of James Burchell AB, who returned on board this afteroon.

Friday, January 17, 1868. Pernambuco
The fines of Richard Rawley AB have been rescinded, he not having been on the Articles and a Ringleader of discontent and a worthless character in every respect. We feel very glad to be rid of him at any cost, he not having any wages due him.

Friday, January 17, 1868. Pernambuco
Noon.

Today the doctor from the British Hospital has been on board and examined John Smith's AB ankles and pronounced them both slightly fractured and recommended his removal to the hospital on Sunday morning, being the first opportunity.

Sunday, January 19, 1868. Pernambuco

This morning sent John Smith AB to shore to the British Hospital according to the doctor's order.

Wednesday, January 29th, 1868. Pernambuco

10 a.m.

This day shipped John Muncaster, AB, to be on board to work tomorrow at 6 o'clock.

Friday, February 21, 1868. Pernambuco

Noon.

John Smith returned from the hospital, but very much crippled, not able to move above but with great difficulty. Scarcely able to work.

Saturday, February 29, 1868. Pernambuco

11 a.m.

This day shipped C. Carlson AB to be on board to work tomorrow morning at 6 o'clock.

Monday, March 2, 1868. Pernambuco

10 a.m.

This day shipped Geo. Williams AB to be on board to work tomorrow morning at 6 o'clock.

Friday, March 6, 1868. Pernambuco

Ship in the stream. All ready to sail for L'pool. Charles Anderson AB begged a passage. Offered to work at 1/– per month. Signed Articles of Agreement accordingly.

Friday, March 6, 1868

2 p.m.

Sailed from Pernambuco for Liverpool.

Friday, March 6, 1868. Off Pernambuco 12 miles

6 p.m.

Discovered a stowaway who gives the name of George Charly. Proceeded on the voyage.

Saturday, March 7, 1868

John Smith AB not being fit for duty on account of his feet, kept him on day duty, only repairing sails, etc.

Saturday, April 4, 1868. Irish Channel

Noon.

Since the times of last entries respecting James Burchell AB he has by his good conduct given no occasion for complaint. I therefore rescind all the former fines entered in this book against him in presence of Wm. Berry, Mate.

Voyage from Liverpool to the Brazils

(The list of crew is missing. From the crew mentioned in the character report attached to the ship's log William Berry again enlisted as mate, John Walker Hardwicke as boatswain, Thomas Doran as carpenter, all other crew members being new. George Pepperell again was master.)

Entries from the Official Log

Wednesday, June 3, 1868. Off Point Lynas

8 p.m.

Discovered we had a stranger Boy on board named John Higgins, a Stowaway.

Sunday, August 2, 1868. Bahia

8 a.m.

The market Boat having been sent up shore as usual with Arthur Woodward (one of the Apprentices), the boat returned without him, he telling the others who were in the boat with him that he was going to leave the Ship and now (that) he had a good chance would avail himself of it at the same time taking the money with him from one of the other Apprentices which he (the other Apprentice) had to buy fruit and vegetables with for the Ship's Company.

Wednesday, August 5, 1868. Bahia

11 a.m.

On receiving information that H.B.M's Consul wished to see me I repaired to the Consulate forthwith. Found that the Boy, Arthur Woodward, had been there on the Monday morning stating that he had been turned out of the Ship. On hearing which, the Consul gave him a letter for me requesting my attendance, which letter he destroyed, and on the following morning again presented himself at the Consulate stating that he had been off to the Ship and that he was not allowed to come on board but had delivered the letter. The Consul again gave him another letter demanding my attendance immediately to answer the charges, which was also destroyed like the first, shortly after which he (Arthur Woodward) returned and told the Consul that he had delivered the letter and (that) my answer was that I was too busy and had other business to attend to and would, when finished, attend to the Consul.

This morning on stating to the Consul that I had not received either of the letters, he told me to bring him (the Boy) before him, which I accordingly did, finding him in a boarding house. When brought before the Consul by me (and) charged with running away and the former charges, viz. theft and falsehood, he had nothing to say in his defence, only that some sailors had given him grog and told him what to say. The Boy being an Apprentice and according to the Consul's orders, took him on board and locked him in a room on Bread and Water for four days.

Friday, August 7, 1868. Bahia

10.30 a.m.

James Butler was so drunk that he was unfit for work. Employed a man in his room, after which he became so abusive and violent that he was put in Irons untill (sic) sober. Returned the following morning to his duty with promises of future better conduct.

Sunday, August 30, 1868. Entering the Port of Paraíba
Whilst entering the port in charge of a licensed pilot and when the ship was in stays, she struck the Fort of Cabedillo with such force as to carry away the rudder making it totally unfit for use, whereby the ship was obliged to be anchored and was detained until the same was repaired.

This Entry has been made in consequence of a false entry having been made in the ship's Log Book, the Mate being off duty at the time the accident occurred.

Tuesday, September 22, 1868. Paraíba
This morning in turning men to their work found that David Lewis AB, Thos. Sykes AB, Joseph Rae AB, Jas. Butler AB and J. Ryan AB were absent from the Ship on shore without leave, their liberty being expired yesterday morning. Put on substitutes in their room.

Wednesday, September 23, 1868. Paraíba
This morning Thos. Sykes AB, Jas. Butler AB, and J. Ryan AB, were still off duty. Employed men in their room.

January 5, 1869 to July 16, 1869

Voyage from Liverpool to Bahia

and any places in the Brazils, West Indies and United States thence to a port for orders and a final port of discharge in the United Kingdom.

Master and Crew

Name	Age	Place of Birth	Rank	Place of discharge/desertion
George Pepperell	30	Dartmouth	Master	Liverpool (Remains)
William George Gover	35	Grimsby	Mate	Liverpool
Charles Covins	25	Liverpool	Boatswain	Liverpool
Thomas Doran	26	Down	Carpenter	Liverpool
Paul Ord	38	New York	Steward	Bahia
Henry Ford	29	Plymouth	Cook	Liverpool
Thomas Middleton Leatherbarrow	20	Liverpool	AB	Liverpool
Thomas Kinrade	37	Liverpool	AB	Liverpool
Joseph McMahon	23	Liverpool	AB	Liverpool
John Muller	27	Sweden	AB	Liverpool
John Williams	32	Corfu	AB	Bahia
William Burns	48	Dublin	AB	Liverpool
William Foster	23	Liverpool	OS	Maceió

James Trisal	23	New York	OS	Bahia
William Killey	20	Liverpool	Supercargo	Liverpool
Richard Seal	33	Bahia	OS	Bahia
John Higgins	13	Manchester	Boy	Liverpool

Apprentices

David Hay

William Easterbrook

Entries from the Official Log

Monday, January 11, 1869. Liverpool

The Ship being ready for sea the lst Mate informed the Crew (as he had done since the time of their being on board, specified in the Articles of Agreement) to be down and commence work tomorrow morning at 6 a.m. according to the said agreement, the Ship being ready to be hauled to the Basin at Tide Time to proceed to sea.

Tuesday, January 12, 1869. Liverpool.

The lst Mate Mr. Gover, 2nd Mate Mr. Covins, Paul Ord Steward, Harry Ford Cook, Thos. Doran Carpenter and James Trisal OS with the two Apprentices and Richard Seal were all the Crew that were on board at the time ordered by the Mate to be on board and commence work at Tide Time. The remainder of the Crew not being on board, engaged 6 Riggers to take the ship to the Pier Head in room of Thomas M. Leatherbarrow AB, Thomas Kinrade AB, Joseph McMahon AB, John Muller AB, John Williams AB, William Burns AB and James Foster, OS. When the Ship was at the Pier Head those men joined. Took steam and proceeded to Sea.

Wednesday, January 13, 1869. St. George's Channel
Today finding all the Seamen wearing Sheath Knives contrary to the regulations for maintaining discipline sanctioned by the Board of Trade No. 1 to 22, I called their attention to the said Article No. 8 and told them (that) after this date I should inflict the fine if I again saw anyone wearing such. I (had) also cautioned them distinctly against doing so before they signed the Articles of Agreement and told them that they could all obtain Knives (clasp) at the same price as on the shore on board the Ship in case they were not provided with them. Viz. l/– each.

Thursday, January 14, 1869. St. George's Channel
John Muller AB again came on deck with a Sheath Knife in his belt. I ordered him to discontinue wearing the same, telling him he was incurring a fine for so doing.

Thursday, January 14, 1869. St. George's Channel
John Williams AB of a breach of Reg. No. 8 for wearing a Sheath Knife.

Fine, one day's pay, £0 – 1 – 8.

William Burns, AB, of a breach of Reg. No. 8, wearing a Sheath Knife.

Fine, one day's pay £0 − 1 − 8.

Thos. M. Leatherbarrow, AB, of a breach of Reg. No. 8, wearing a Sheath Knife,

One day's pay, £0 − 1 − 8.

Friday, January 14, 1869. St George's Channel
Heavy SW gales and thick dirty weather. Since leaving Liverpool experienced very heavy weather, washing away the Coat of the Bowsprit and the Hause Choc Rings, the Chains being bent. The Forecastle through the stress of weather became uninhabitable. Ordered the Crew Aft in the Fore Cabin untill (sic) an opportunity offered for the Carpenter to make the same perfectly water tight. Cautioned the Crew against smoking below, it being contrary to the Regulation 1 to 22 for maintaining discipline sanctioned by the Board of Trade.

Friday, January 15, 1869. St. George's Channel
John Muller AB still persists in wearing a Sheath Knife.

Fine, one day's pay, £0 − 1 − 8.

Also for a breach of Reg. No. 13, smoking below, one day's pay, £0 − 1 − 8.

Friday, January 15, 1869. St. George's Channel
Thos. M. Leatherbarrow, AB. Same offence in both clauses wearing a Sheath Knife.

One day's pay, £0 – 1 – 8.

Smoking below, one day's pay, £0 – 1 – 8.

Sunday, January 17, 1869

John Muller AB came aft at noon, the only one of the Crew, with a piece of Pudding, asking me if that was enough for a man to work upon. I told him it was his allowance, whereon he became very insolent and said he did not come here to be humbugged. Insolence and Contemptuous Language to the Master, on this occasion interlading his discourse or complaint with oaths, and not as in the Agreement to make his complaint "in a quiet orderly manner". Nevertheless, I took such steps to see the allowance issued out accordingly.

Insolence and Contemptuous Language to the Master, one day's pay, £0 – 1 – 8.

Not being washed and shaved, one day's pay, £0 – 1 – 8.

This being the only man who has made any complaint, we are of opinion that the same John Muller AB is a discontented man, scarcely ever civil to the Officer of watch, Mr. Covins, and we are furthermore of (the) opinion that he is ready to make a disturbance in the Vessel (at) the first opportunity he has of doing so.

Thursday, January 21, 1869

The weather having now become fine and the Forecastle being thoroughly caulked and perfectly watertight, I ordered the Crew forward into their respective part of the Vessel. Notwithstanding the cautions I have given them, they have continued to smoke below ever since they have been located in the Fore Cabin.

Saturday, January 23, 1869
Noon.

Staying ship I ordered John Muller AB to make fast the wheel and give a pull in the Main Brace. He refused duty by not obeying my orders and became insolent in the extreme, telling me he did not come here to be bounced on and being very abusive. I told him to keep quiet or I should put him in Irons. He replied (that) he did not care. But by the time the ship was round he went to the pulling of the ropes, and on coming back to the wheel he told me (that) he did not care. I may write just as much as I pleased. He would get the better of any law, he being a foreigner. He has often tried to aggravate me to strike him so that he may have the law for me, and he has also made his boast (that) if the Captain would strike him he would make him pay dear. He certainly says almost what he thinks proper and I am obliged to put up with it. But we (the Officers) are quite satisfied that he has shown himself to be discontented and has often endeavoured to promote a quarrel.

Saturday, January 21, 1869
　8 a.m.

Starboard watch on deck in charge of 2nd Mate Mr. Covins. Ordered 2 of the watch, Thos. M. Leatherbarrow and John Muller, aloft to scrape the Mizzen Mast. They went very slowly about their work and frequently talking and laughing at the same time. A Boy, A. Hay, was placed half way down the mast to scrape the half. Observing how very lazy they, the two men, were and that the Boy had done his half, I ordered it to be finished before they went below. But at 8 o'clock they came down, contrary to my orders, given through the 2nd Mate and given to them by him. They told him (that) they were going to their breakfast. As soon as I became aware of the fact I sent for them in presence of my officers and asked them why they had disobeyed my orders when they distinctly told me (that) they would not do it. I read them that part of the Agreement wherein it says, "They shall be obedient at all times to the lawful commands of the said Master", telling them (that) if they still refused duty I should be obliged to confine them and put them in Irons. The mast would have been finished in half an hour if they had gone about it, or it could easily have been finished by 8 o'clock, seeing (that) the Boy (had) done his half, and only a Boy against two Able Bodied Seamen. But they would not, this man John Muller leading the other. He has ever been since joining the ship a lazy saucy, foul-spoken man and was only waiting for something to turn to commence a rebellion. As they still persist in disobeying lawful commands have put them both in confinement, handcuffed, using no violence whatever.

Saturday, 20 February, 1869

John Muller and Thos. M. Leatherbarrow still refuse to go to their duty. Have put them on short allowance. Viz: l½ lbs. bread and 1 quart water, everyone else on 2 quarts of water, on account of our tank leaking out.

Monday, February 22, 1869

10 a.m.

Called both prisoners aft, and in the presence of the Mate read the charges distinctly over to them. (Thos. M. Leatherbarrow returns to his duty at noon.) The both prisoners declinging having anything to say respecting the foregoing charges, acknowledging the same to be correct.

Saturday, February 27, 1869

The Ship's Company being on short allowance of water, I issued out 2 pt. Bottles of Ale to each man. The Steward, Paul Ord became intoxicated about tea time, performing his duty in a very unsatisfactory manner. On my finding him in this state I discovered some Ale missing from the Cabin which, when I accused him of taking, he denied throwing anything about. But one thing I am certain of, he was Intoxicated. This being the first offence coming under our notice (with the exception of the two first days after sailing from Liverpool) and under these circumstances, viz: of being on a short allowance of water, have not imposed the fine, but have cautioned him accordingly, he on his part promising to become a Teetotaller.

Saturday, March 20, 1869. Bahia

About 5 p.m. after being on shore on Ship's business came on board and found Paul Ord, Steward, again intoxicated and quarrelsome with the Mate, Mr. Gover, neglecting his duty in clearing away and washing up his Tea things (and) leaving everything in a disorderly state. Again cautioned on the following day, he promising amendment.

Thursday, April 15, 1869. Bahia

About 2 p.m. came on board the Ship to shift into the loading ground. Again found the Steward, Paul Ord intoxicated, he having served me so. Before I have kept all spirits locked up, but by some means he must in our opinion have obtained my keys to become so. After another caution, (after) the next offence I shall most certainly punish (him). I have again accepted his promised amendment.

Sunday, April 18, 1869. Bahia

Paul Ord, Steward, again drunk and utterly incapable. Dinner an hour late, and when said to be ready found everything very dirty. In fact, things just as they had been used at breakfast time brought on the table. After bringing the soup he disappeared and shortly after was discovered laying on some sails in the Fore Cabin, leaving myself and officers to get dinner the best we could with dirty plates, knives and forks, etc. etc. In fact, not able to find half the necessary utensils to get dinner with. He also destroyed by his carelessness whilst being in this state a large quantity of plates and other crockery ware.

Monday, April 19, 1869. Bahia

Again the Steward, Paul Ord drunk and incapable, he doing his duty up to 1 p.m. when he brought the soup on the Table for dinner and then knocked off, going to lay down in the Half Deck. Obliged to call the Cook from his work to bring the dinner aft and attend, this being the fourth time of his being in this state since being in this port and once at sea, and after repeated cautions to him of the consequences of this was repeated, and he as often promising amendment. I have from this date disrated him from being Steward, he proving himself not trustworthy, finding also a great many things have been destroyed while in this state, his expenditure book for stores not having been kept up since the 4th April (the 2nd Mate then filling them up), he not keeping any account of provisions coming off from the shore for daily use, and in fact neglecting other portions of his duty. I have turned him out of the Cabin, he keeping the first anchor watch, the same as another of the Crew.

Tuesday, April 21, 1869. Bahia

This morning at 6 o'clock ordered Paul Ord to work with the rest of the Crew. When he refused saying he could not do sailor's work, the Mate, Mr. Gover, ordered him, also myself, at the same time telling him that he was not wanted to do sailor's work but to work. Sailors and labourers employed all day passing sugar. As everyone was busy put him in Irons, there being no person to look after him, four of the Crew being sick and one Officer on shore tallying cargos. At 2 p.m. again ordered him to work. He still refused. At 6 p.m.let him out of Irons, but gave him bread and water and since his refusal feel only justified in inflicting the whole of the Fines No. 9 embodied in the Regulations for preserving discipline sanctioned by the Board of Trade, viz: After the first offence, two days pay for each case of Drunkennes.

For 4 times drunk, 2 days pay each

For refusal to work on lawful command, 2 days pay.

July 14, 1869. Arrived at Liverpool

All those foregoing entries entered in this Log against breach of discipline committed on board during the voyage are hereby rescinded owing to their good conduct the latter portion of the voyage.

Paul Ord, Steward, John Williams AB, and James Trisal OS, were discharged before the British Consul at Bahia.

September 23, 1869 to April 9, 1870

Voyage from Liverpool to Bahia

and any ports and places in the Brazils and United States, and back to a final port of discharge in the United Kingdom. Term not to exceed 12 months.

Master and Crew

Name	Age	Place of Birth	Rank	Place of discharge/desertion
George Pepperell	30	Devon	Master	Liverpool (Remains)
William George Gover	39	Grimsby	Mate	Liverpool
Albert Jones	29	Heliogoland	Boatswain	Liverpool
Thomas Doran	26	Down	Carpenter	Liverpool
Thomas Higginson	26	Manchester	Steward	Liverpool
Alexander Bolitho	26	Padstow	Cook	Liverpool
John Martin	30	Fowey	AB	Liverpool
Alfred Isaac	38	Troon	AB	Liverpool
William Smith	36	Jersey	AB	Bahia (deserted)
Dennis Brennan	22	Limerick	AB	Did not board
William Antonio	38	Brest	AB	Bahia (deserted)
William Haswell	18	Dublin	OS	Liverpool
William Saulters	19	Belfast	OS	Liverpool
Francis Rogers	25	Mexico	AB	Bahia (deserted)

Enlisted at Bahia

John Mulchahy	19	Bristol	AB	
Charles Leemann	36	Norway	AB	
Francis Rogers	25	Mexico	AB	Did not board

Apprentices

David Alexander Hay	16		Deserted
William Easterbrook	15		

Entries from the Official Log

(Undated)

Articles of Agreement signed for the Crew to be on board the 23rd inst. the Ship not going to sea, the Crew did not join until the 24th inst. from which date their wages commenced.

(Undated)

All the Crew on board but Dennis Brennan AB. Shipped Francis Rogers AB, in his stead and proceeded to sea.

Thursday, October 14, 1869

7 p.m.

The starboard watch on deck from 6 p.m. to 8 p.m. which consists of William Smith AB, William Antonio AB, Francis Rogers OS, and William Haswell OS, in charge of Albert Jones Boatswain in lieu of 2nd Mate. The Boatswain called the watch aft to empty some water from a Tub into a Cask. I at the time walking the deck heard a deal of grumbling and Insolence. I called the watch aft to know what the matter was, when the said William Smith answered very insolently (that) he was not going to be humbugged by anybody. I warned him that he had better behave himself and obey all the lawful commands given him by those Officers appointed over him and referred them to the copy of the Articles of Agreement wherein it is specified "that the said crew shall at <u>all</u> times be obedient to the lawful commands of the said Officers". His conduct was both insolent and impertinent as also (was) Wm. Antonio AB and Francis Rogers OS. I then gave some orders which they eventually obeyed, but Wm. Smith AB assured me (that) I may carry him to Monte Video (sic) or anywhere I was going to in Irons if I liked. It was all the same to him.

Friday, October 15, 1869.

Things going on as usual on board. The aforesaid William Smith AB appearing very discontented, and he (was) evidently leading the other members of the watch, and although warned that it is against the Articles established by the Board of Trade for maintaining discipline on board ship, viz: of wearing a Sheath Knife, he persists in wearing a Clasp Knife open in a sheath, thus converting the same into a Sheath Knife, the most of the others following his example.

Saturday, November 13, 1869. Bahia.

At 6.30 p.m. came to anchor in the Franquia Ground of the Port of Bahia.

Monday, November 15, 1869. Franquia Ground, Bahia.

Whilst I was walking the deck (at) about 1.30 p.m. William Smith AB came on the Poop and addressed me as follows. "Here, what is the reason you don't give us pork for our rations while there is plenty of it in the ship? Cause if you don't give us pork with pea soup I ain't going to do any more work in this 'ere ship." I told him I had given him beef as a substitute which the Articles specify thus, that beef can be substituted for pork or pork for beef. Presently another came Aft, Alfred Isaac, and asked if the men could have pork. As he came in a most proper manner and orderly I explained to him that I had intended to give them fresh beef, but (the Ship) laying such a long way down (in the harbour) and having to shift the ship by order of the Harbour Master I could not make it convenient to send the boat with hands away to the market. But at the earliest part of the voyage more pork had been used than beef. I (therefore) thought it a good opportunity of equallising (sic) the salt provisions and also that the fresh beef obtained being of a very dry nature an allowance of salt pork occasionally would be an improvement. Finding the greater part of the Crew dissatisfied I called all hands aft to know there (sic) complaints, when William Smith AB, William Antonio AB (who did not come,(thus) disobeying orders), John Martin AB and Francis Rogers OS refused to do any more duty in the Ship. Although the Harbour Master had ordered us to shift our berth at 6.30 p.m. and all hands called to pump the Ship, the Ship making a little water, they refused, as also at 8 p.m. When ordered to keep an anchor watch they still refused, and it is our candid beleif (sic) that William Smith AB is the ringleader and stirer-up of this Insubordination, their intention being to get clear of the Ship, as they all of them shifted from their working clothes and packed up all their effects.

Tuesday, November 16, 1869. Bahia.

At 6 a.m. the hands were called to discharge Gunpowder, a portion of the cargo, when the same men as yesterday refused still to do any more duty. The Vessel had soon to discharge about 10 tons of Gunpowder and remove into the discharging ground under a fine of 1000,000 Milries. These men who are a portion of the Crew, and a large portion, still refuse, whatever the consequences may be. By dint of great perseverence on the part of the remaining portion of the Crew with myself, succeeded in performing the both, these men sitting and looking on the while, no doubt by so doing trying to provoke a quarrel which is an additional punishable offence. If they had continued at their work untill (sic) the Ship was moored in a safe berth the offence would not in our opinion have been so gross. But they have persisted in refusal (in) spite of any consequences that may ensue and only feel justified in punishing them to the utmost of the Law.

Sunday, November 21, 1869. Bahia.

Noon.

This morning having been on shore to the English Church before going I locked up all Spirits. This proceeding so annoyed Thos. Higginson Steward, that he said that whenever he had the chance he would get grog. Have seen him being on some occasions a little the worse for Drink, so that I do not consider him trustworthy. But although I locked the spirit locker he with another key opened it and helped himself, this he acknowledged to me, as when I returned on board I found the locker had been opened. Since he has been in the Ship he has had a glass of rum every night with the officers.

Wednesday, November 24, 1869. Bahia.

10 a.m.

The Crew who refused duty and have been kept in jail for refusal have today been ordered on board by H.B.M's Consul.

Wednesday, November 24, 1869. Bahia.

5.30 p.m.

On coming on board I found the Steward Thos. Higginson the worse for Drink, he having during my absence been helping himself. He came to me and asked for his discharge which on being refused became very insolent. I find that whenever he gets drink he becomes Insolent and discontented, the Ship being too small as well as his wages (being too little). Although he signed the Agreement for the sum stipulated against his name, his manner has been throughout very abrupt, everything seeming a trouble to him if told he had to do it, omitting to do many things as part of his duty.

Friday, November 26, 1869.

Finding neither of the men had joined the Ship have today reported the same to H.B.M.'s Consul as deserted. Their names are Wm. Smith AB, Wm. Antonio AB, Francis Rogers OS, John Martin AB.

Friday, December 3, 1869. Bahia.

Again came on board and found Thos. Higginson, Steward, intoxicated. I was obliged to trim the Cabin lamp, fearful of some accident occurring, it being a parafin lamp. Seeing he was drunk and hearing him breaking crockeryware I ordered him to leave the pantry and (go) to to bed. He again asked for his discharge, but seeing he was drunk I took no notice of him and went on deck to avoid any noise.

Wednesday, December 8, 1869. Bahia.

This being an holiday Thos. Higginson came to me and asked for liberty to go on shore which I granted him. He came on board sometime during the night. I have reason to beleive (sic) he brought Grog into the Ship. The following day he was again the worse for drink, he inviting the carpenter whilst at their work to leave it and come into the (deck) House and have some drink with him.

Saturday, December 11, 1869. Bahia.

Again on coming on board this evening I find Thos. Higginson in Drink. During the time I was at Tea he became very insolent and finding my temper could not stand any more for I really beleive he was trying to excite me to strike him, I ordered him on deck. At the time I did so not intending to put him out of the Cabin but to send him away untill (sic) such time as my temper had cooled down. As he refused to go when ordered untill (sic) threatened with being put in Irons, after a short time I called him to me, when he told me he would not take his discharge even if I would give it him, which I have never thought of doing, but he asked me to let (him) go forward and to be from this a.m. Ordinary Seaman. I ordered him to his work untill (sic) Monday when I would take him before the British Consul who would hear his case and give the redress it demanded, which he again refused.

Monday, December 13, 1869. Bahia.

5.30 a.m.

Mr Gover, lst. Mate, with myself consider Thos. Higginson no longer fit to be Steward, he having been found drunk (on) five different occasions. At such times he becomes very Insolent, and at his <u>own request</u> have allowed him to go forward and as he promised to do all he could have disrated him from being Steward since his refusal of duty on Saturday night, and now consider him to be an Ordinary Seaman. Seeing that he has gone forward on his account and had sufficient time to consider the course he has adopted I am determined not to take him back as Steward on any account, and we are further of (the) opinion that he has caused a great deal of discontent amongst the crew, for whatever is said in the Cabin soon becomes known throughout the Ship through him.

Thursday, December 23, 1869. Bahia.

Today one of the aforenamed seamen, John Martin AS who deserted the Ship on the 24th ultimo has been again allowed to join being in a state of destitution on Shore and begged to be allowed to be taken on the ship again, the other three having left the ship with the determination of deserting as they each one put extra suits of clothing before leaving.

Tuesday, St. John's Day, December 28, 1869. Bahia.

At the request of Thos. Higginson I allowed him to go to the British Consul. He wanted advice and redress which he says he cannot get. He has gone back to his work which at his own request he is now doing. He wants now to come back into the Cabin which I again refused, for after carefully weighing the matter over I consider (that) his conduct has been so unsatisfactory that although able to do his work he would only do it when he thought proper and (only) as much as he considered equal to the wages he was paid, for ever since he joined the ship he has never attempted to clean the Arms and the Mahogany of which the Cabin is composed. The latter he has dusted about once a week which ought to have been done once a day, the Arms cleaned and the Mahogany cleaned with furniture paste once a week and (more) frequently since lying in Bahia. Although he (only) had three pairs of boots of mine to clean I have had to go on shore with a dirty pair. I have in fact been obliged to keep him (as) Steward for some time longer than I at first thought of doing, being so short-handed, and to give him an opportunity of amending his conduct. But now of his own free will and request having gone forward with the crew and become an Ordinary Seaman I cannot think of taking him back. He proving himself incompetent through drink on five occasions, being insolent and impertinent, and since he has gone forward we have found that this man has been the primary cause of a great deal of dissatisfaction amongst the Ship's Company, he having at different times reported to them that he had a great deal to do to get for them their regular allowance which has always been a trouble to him to weigh out to them, professing to give them their rations by guess and a larger portion than the allowance.

Tuesday, February 15, 1870. Bahia.

Chas. Leemann has this day shipped as AB to join this Ship on the 16th Feby. 1870.

Thursday, February 17, 1870. Bahia.

John Mulcahy has this day been shipped as AB to be on board tomorrow.

Monday February 21, 1870. Bahia.

Francis Rogers OS has this day been shipped as one of the Crew, but up to 5 p.m., he not having made his appearance, the Ship has left without him.

Thursday, February 17, 1870. Bahia.

All the entries against Thos. Higginson have this day been distinctly read over to the said Thos. Higginson according to the Act (before the ship leaving port) in presence of the Mate and H.B.M's Consul and myself at the Consulate of Bahia. The said Thos. Higginson refusing to make any statement, his only answer is that the entries are greatly exaggerated and he will reserve his evidence untill (sic) he gets to L'pool.

Friday, April 5, 1870. Liverpool.

It is mutually agreed today between Thos. Higginson and myself the Master that the said Thos. Higginson shall receive wages at the rate of £2 10 0 per month since his having done his duty as Seaman, and his conduct has been satisfactory.

(Undated) Liverpool.

The conduct of John Martin AB since he has again joined the Ship has been throughout satisfactory up to the end of the voyage.

Voyage from Liverpool to Pernambuco

and any port in the Brazils and back to the United Kingdom.

Master and Crew

Name	Rank
(George Pepperell)	Master
William G. Gover	Mate
Albert Jones	Boatswain
Andrew Albert	Carpenter
Alexander Bolitho	Cook
David Winder	AB
William Lloyd	AB
James Bailey	AB
Samuel Balmforth	AB
Joseph Reynolds	AB
George B. Mitchelson	OS
John Crossly	OS

Apprentices

William Johnson
John Payne
James Payne

Entries from the Official Log (Incomplete)

Saturday, July 9, 1870. Pernambuco.

11 a.m.

This day have paid off the Two Boys by mutual consent at the British Consulate before the Vice Consul.

Monday, July 11, 1870. Pernambuco.

6 a.m.

On turning the hands to work this morning found that Samuel Balmforth AB and Geo. B. Mitchelson OS had left the Ship during the night taking all their effects with them.

Wednesday. (Undated) Pernambuco.

6 p.m.

Today have left Pernambuco and the two above named Seamen not on board. Now consider them deserters.

Voyage from Liverpool to New Calabar

and back to a final port of discharge in the United Kingdom. Term not to exceed 12 months.

Master and Crew

Name	Age	Place of Birth	Rank	Place of discharge/desertion
Stephen Goodman	58	Whitehaven	Master	New Calabar
Heinrich Johann Albert	25	Prussia	Mate	Left behind (in Liverpool) by mutual consent to give evidence in case of collision
George Ayer	42	Liverpool	Boatswain	Transferred to another ship at Opobo
Charles McCoombe	32	Liverpool	Carpenter	Liverpool
Thomas Bowyer	31	Liverpool	Carpenter	Liverpool
Peter Roebuck	37	Liverpool	Steward	Transferred at New Calabar to George Washington
George Franklin Baker	37	Massachuset	Cook	Liverpool
James McGill	21	Lurgan	AB	Transferred at New Calabar to George Washington
Thomas Barry	22	St. John, N.B.	AB	New Calabar – died
John Peterson	26	London	AB	Liverpool

John Valentine	25	Liverpool	AB	Did not board
Alexander Branch	26	Jamaica	AB	Transferred at New Calabar to George Washington
Charles Llewellyn	40	St. Vincent	AB	Transferred to George Washington
Robert Mowbray	29	Glasgow	AB	Did not board
Adam Louis Murray	16	Brest	OS	Transferred to George Washington
William Barrow	21	Cheshire	OS	Did not board
Edward Jennings Gibson	50	Plymouth	Mate	Died at sea
Peter Anseu	36	St. John	AB	Transferred to George Washington
John Dunstan Braily	50	Falmouth	AB	Liverpool
Charles Gage	18	London	OS	Liverpool
Thomas Power	23	Waterford	AB	Transferred to George Washington
Henry Challoner	18	Liverpool	OS	Liverpool

Enlisted at New Calabar

John Campbell	60	Jamaica	Master	Liverpool (Remains)
John Kelly	35	Cork	AB	Liverpool
John Costello	20	New York	AB	Liverpool
John Thomas	21	Liverpool	OS	Liverpool
Francis Timms	21	Leeward Islands	AB	Liverpool
Henry Bradbury	20	Birmingham	OS	Liverpool
David Salmon	28	Milfordhaven	Boatswain	Liverpool

Thomas Lynch	21	Liverpool		AB	Liverpool
John Martin	42	Calcutta		Steward	Liverpool

Entries from the Official Log

Friday, July 14, 1871. New Calabar, Africa.

At 1 p.m. Captain Stephen Goodman left the ship and proceeded to Bonny river to go as passenger to Liverpool by the Barque "George Washington".

Friday, November 24, 1871. New Calabar, Africa.

At 2.45 p.m. Thomas Barry AB departed this life after a lingering Illness since July 25th, attended continually by the doctor of the Port. After the Carpenter had made a coffin took the body to Snake Island and at 7 p.m. he was respectably interred by me, Edward Jennings Gibson, Chief Officer, Charles McCoombe, Carpenter, and Dunstan Brady AB.

December 15, 1871. New Calabar, Africa.

The effects of Thomas Barry AB, late deceased, was this day sold and realized the sum of £1 7 0

February 25, 1872. (At sea)

Edward Jennings Gibson, Chief Officer departed this life at 1.30 a.m. suffering for some time with debility and old age. At duty for a few days and off duty at intervals taking on medicine, soups, arrowroot.

Voyage from Liverpool to the West Coast of Africa

to trade in any ports, bays and rivers, there and back to a final port of discharge in the United Kingdom. Term not to exceed 3 years.

Master and Crew

Name	Age	Place of Birth	Rank	Place of discharge/desertion
John Campbell	60	Jamaica	Master	New Calabar
William McLean	33	Dumfries	Mate	New Calabar
Daniel Shaw	46	Devon	Boatswain	New Calabar
(Name illegible)	38	Sweden	Carpenter	New Calabar
John Flanagan	36	Liverpool	Cook	New Calabar
John Martin	42	Calcutta	Steward	New Calabar
John Johnson	33	Madagascar	?	New Calabar
(Name illegible)	27	France	AB	New Calabar
William Brown	40	Liverpool	AB	New Calabar
James Davis	30	St. Helena	AB	New Calabar
Bernard Gerraty	20	Liverpool	AB	New Calabar
Thomas Hughes	23	Liverpool	AB	New Calabar
John (?)	27	London	AB	New Calabar

James Custer	38	London	AB	New Calabar
Benjamin Lory	34	London	AB	New Calabar
James Brown	21	Liverpool	OS	Did not board
Richard Hayes	19	Dublin	OS	New Calabar
James Williams	18	Sunderland	OS	New Calabar
Robert Oliver	26	Australia	OS	New Calabar

(All crew including master were discharged and transferred to other ships at New Calabar – the carpenter, cook, steward and and six others in July, the master, mate and remaining six in October 1872. There appears to exist no entries to the log book.

On January 27, 1880 it is stated on the Agreement and Account of Crew that Mimosa was converted to a hulk.)

Mimosa's Voyages, a companion volume to *Mimosa: The life and times of the ship that sailed to Patagonia,* is just one of a whole range of publications from Y Lolfa. For a full list of books currently in print, send now for your free copy of our new full-colour catalogue. Or simply surf into our website

www.ylolfa.com

for secure on-line ordering.

TALYBONT CEREDIGION CYMRU SY24 5AP
e-mail ylolfa@ylolfa.com
website www.ylolfa.com